# *just* Peachy

**Belinda Smith-Sullivan**

*Photographs by*

MARK BOUGHTON

**GIBBS SMITH**

TO ENRICH AND INSPIRE HUMANKIND

The writing and photography in this book evoke the beauty and aroma of real peaches as Chef Belinda shares the experiences of the childhood summers spent in the Mississippi Delta that ignited her love for the fruit. Now living in the heart of South Carolina peach country, she has compiled this extensive collection of sweet and savory peach recipes to make you eat and enjoy them.

*—Nathalie Dupree*

James Beard Award Winner for *Mastering the Art of Southern Cooking*

With recipes that range from sweet to savory and will take you from morning to night, peaches take the main stage in *Just Peachy*. This delightful cookbook is full of stunning photographs; valuable, practical information about the South's signature fruit; and a bushel basket full of tantalizing, go-to recipes. It's an absolute masterpeach!

*—Virginia Willis*

James Beard Award-winning cookbook author and chef

*Just Peachy* is visually stunning, innovative, and jam-packed with creative peach-inspired recipes—making it the go-to cookbook for all things peach!

*—Chef Jennifer Hill Booker*

These are no ordinary peach recipes because Belinda is no ordinary author. This chef, product developer, food writer, culinary authority, airplane pilot, and sweet friend to many, doesn't do anything halfway! Her bubbly personality and knowledgeable voice are ever-present throughout each and every page. Her stories offer a delightful glimpse into heartwarming family memories, deep personal friendships, and international experience. Her mouthwatering recipes tantalize the palate with delicious, fresh, and comforting flavors. I can't wait to cook my way through each page of this book again and again.

*—Sandra A. Gutierrez*

Award-Winning Author of *Empanadas: The Hand-Held Pies of Latin America*

There is nothing quite like a fresh peach—they just drip with the essence of a well-spent summer. Belinda's mouthwatering Cast Iron Peach Cornbread and Peach Bourbon Roast Chicken are just two of the recipes in this delightful ode to my favorite fruit that I know will be a mainstay on our dinner table.

*—Carrie Morey*

Founder of Callie's Charleston Biscuits and Callie's Hot Little Biscuit

First Edition
23 22 21 20 19      5 4 3 2 1

Text © 2019 Belinda Smith-Sullivan
Photographs © 2019 Mark Boughton
Teresa Blackburn Food and Prop Stylist
Tonya Whitaker Food Assistant

Published by
Gibbs Smith
P.O. Box 667
Layton, Utah 84041

1.800.835.4993 orders
www.gibbs-smith.com

Designed by Rita Sowins / Sowins Design
Printed and bound in Hong Kong

Gibbs Smith books are printed on either recycled, 100% post-consumer waste, FSC-certified papers or on paper produced from sustainable PEFC-certified forest/controlled wood source. Learn more at www.pefc.org.

Library of Congress Cataloging-in-Publication Data
Names: Smith-Sullivan, Belinda, 1949- author. | Boughton, Mark, 1967- photographer.
Title: Just peachy / Belinda Smith-Sullivan ; photographs by Mark Boughton.
Description: First edition. | Layton, Utah : Gibbs Smith, 2019. |
Includes index.
Identifiers: LCCN 2018037048 | ISBN 9781423651260 (jacketless hardcover)
Subjects: LCSH: Peach. | LCGFT: Cookbooks.
Classification: LCC TX813.P4 S65 2019 | DDC 641.6/425--dc23
LC record available at https://lccn.loc.gov/2018037048

To my grandmother Louise, who lit the peach flame in my heart;
and to my mother Naomi, who kept it burning.

# Contents

# Foreword

About fifteen summers ago I arranged to meet two fellow East Coast friends for a morning breakfast meeting at San Francisco's Ferry Building Marketplace, located at the end of Market Street in the shadow of the towering Bay Bridge. I had recently moved to Charlotte, North Carolina, and noticed a new café in the market, owned by Frog Hollow Farm, had opened since my last visit to San Francisco. I had just read about them, about how Alice Waters and Jeffrey Steingarten and pretty much every peach freak I knew were raving about their super high brix peaches. And, since timing is everything, it just happened to be peak season so I grabbed a table while waiting for my friends to arrive and then ordered some coffee and looked over the few remaining peaches in the basket, which were selling for $5.00 a pound! Yikes! But this was my one chance, so I picked out three tree-ripened beauties and brought them to the table just as my friends arrived. I gave them each a peach and we all took a bite. Dead silence—crickets—then sighs of joy and oh-my god as we stared wide-eyed at each other, juice dripping down our chins, and continued to devour our peaches.

After we finished, I went back to the peach basket to get more, but, as I feared, they were already sold out—timing is everything. I returned to the table empty handed. One of my friends said, in a low, almost reverential voice, "Do you get the feeling this was, maybe, the first time any of us ever tasted a real peach and experienced the essence of peachness?"

I recalled that ah-ha moment of *peachness* when I opened the pages of Belinda Smith-Sullivan's gorgeous new book, *Just Peachy*, and let her words lead me back, through her own connectedness to cherished food memories, to that moment in San Francisco when I realized that, yes, there are peaches but, also, that there are *peaches!*

I feel about peaches, as I do about a number of favorite foods, that there are only two kinds: good and very good. That day at the Frog Hollow Farm Café kind of spoiled me for peaches, yet I continue eating them throughout every summer no matter where they are grown, or their stone type, always in search of more such peachy epiphanies.

Belinda is one of the rare culinary students that I've taught who not only can create delicious dishes and food products, but also has a love of words and can write beautifully and passionately about food. It gives me great joy to see all of her talents come together in this, her first—but undoubtedly not her last—book. And I think you, as was I, will be delightfully transported through Belinda's words and recipes (not to mention Mark Boughton's luscious photography), to your own vivid ah-ha moments of taste memory awakenings.

Peter Reinhart, James Beard Award–winning Chef
Charlotte, NC 2018

# Acknowledgments

"If I have seen further, it is by standing on the shoulders of giants!"—Sir Isaac Newton

When I think of all the people who helped get me here, they are many and I am so very grateful. I wish to acknowledge:

Chef Peter Reinhart of Johnson & Wales University for giving me my first food writing opportunities. I hope I have made you proud.

Martha Hopkins of Terrace Partners, my agent, for believing in me and for her patience throughout the proposal writing process.

Dianne Jacob, writing coach extraordinaire, who was an incredible sounding board for helping me refine my book concept.

Michelle Branson and Gibbs Smith for taking a chance on a newcomer.

Nancie McDermott, Sandra Gutierrez, Jamie Schler, and Jill O'Connor for their never-ending friendship, support, and encouragement…I love you all!

*South Carolina Living Magazine* and *Bella Magazine* for providing a platform for me to share my culinary knowledge with readers in South Carolina and beyond. I have enjoyed every minute.

Mark Boughton and Teresa Blackburn for your photography and styling genius. You made this book beautiful.

Lynne Chappell of Chappell Farms for being a "champion" of my book from the inception, and your willingness to share your family's story and recipe. I appreciate you.

Yonce "Big Smile" Peaches for the many hours of consultation, tours of their peach processing facility, and photo opportunities in their peach orchards. I am most grateful.

My husband, Dan, who never doubted for one moment that I could accomplish this goal. And for being my biggest cheerleader every step of the way.

Finally, my faithful Cavalier King Charles Spaniel, Sir Winston, who spent hours napping on my lap while I wrote this book.

Introduction

# "An apple is an excellent thing—until you have tried a peach."—George du Maurier

*M*y love for peaches goes way back.

I live in Edgefield County, South Carolina, the peach capital of the South. But I didn't fall in love with peaches when I moved there. My love affair began much earlier. I spent all of my summers in Charleston, Mississippi, on my grandparents' farm. My grandfather was a cotton sharecropper, like all of the other farmers around him. Since no one had much of anything, bartering was a way of life. If you had an abundance of sweet potatoes and needed tomatoes, you bartered with someone who had an abundance of tomatoes and needed sweet potatoes. That's how it worked, and no one wanted for anything. Neighbors took care of neighbors, and our neighbors delivered bushels of peaches to our doorstep throughout the heat of summer.

My grandmother, cousins, and I would spend hours on the front porch peeling and slicing peaches, getting them ready to be canned and made into preserves or peach brandy. I was then, and am now still, fascinated by the process. I never complained because, if memory serves me, I ate one peach for every two peaches I peeled. My grandmother always turned a blind eye. She was kind like that.

I learned how to cook in my grandmother's modest Mississippi country kitchen, where there was only a wood-burning stove in the middle of the room and a small sink in the corner. There

My grandparents, John L. Batteast and Louise Moore Batteast

was no running water. Every morning, we kids would wake up at 5:30 a.m. to bring water in from the well and wood from the woodpile so that my grandmother could start preparing breakfast. She would stand in the kitchen, dressed and in her apron, her hands on her hips, waiting for her little helpers. With the water and wood delivered to the appropriate places in the kitchen, the boys were off to feed the animals, and Grandmother and I would start the meals of the day. It always amazed me how she cooked both breakfast and dinner at the same time. There would be biscuits and a cake or pie baking side-by-side in the oven, and pots filled with grits and collard greens on top of the stove. My first assignment was to set the table— an old wooden harvest table with mismatched chairs—and to set it with equally mismatched plates, glasses, and forks. The original shabby chic, born out of necessity. The hand-churned butter and homemade peach preserves sat in the middle, like stars of the breakfast table. All that was missing were the big, fat biscuits that would soon be coming out of the oven, which could be improved only with a smear of the sweet cream butter and peach preserves.

The minute I arrived on the farm, I wanted to know if the peaches had come in yet. I was always just a bit early, leaving me impatient until the first round was ripe enough to pick. I was like a broken record that never stopped— my questioning just switched from, "Have they come in yet?" to "Are we getting more peaches

My mother Naomi Batteast Smith and Grandmother Louise Moore Batteast

today?" When my friends back home in Chicago asked me about my summers in Mississippi and what I did on the farm, my enthusiastic response every year was the same: "We canned peaches." I'm vague on many of the other activities that took place on the farm during those summers, but the memory of the taste and the silky texture of those endless peaches never fades.

After my grandparents passed away, summers in Mississippi gave way to road trips to southern Michigan with my mother and aunts. There, we'd make a day at the pick-your-own peach orchards and drive back home to Chicago with a trunk brimming with peaches. When you've got that many peaches, there's nothing to do but use them, and quickly. Just like in Mississippi, my mother and I would start the process of canning the fruit, peeling, chopping, and simmering to release the pectin. It would've made my grandmother proud.

After Mississippi, after Chicago, it didn't matter where I lived. Whenever I came home to visit, I came home to a homemade peach pie from my mother. This tradition ended only with her passing. Nothing, absolutely nothing, evokes the memory of my mother or my grandmother more clearly than a peach pie still warm from the oven. While I have nearly perfected their recipes, I can tell you that mine never seem to taste quite like theirs, and I suspect that they never will.

Since those long-ago summers on the farm with my grandparents, I have spent much of my adult life experimenting with peaches, and my world has expanded well beyond the peach pie and preserves of my youth.

Today, I live in the heart of peach country. (Though my neighbors in Georgia may beg to differ.) The trees along Highway 25 are heavy with fruit as I write this, and those very peaches will be making their way onto cheese boards and into chutneys, fresh salads, chilled soups, and decadent desserts for the rest of the year.

Living in South Carolina is not just about having an abundance of peaches to eat during the summer; it is about taking pride in our most cherished crop. Every few weeks of peach season brings a different variety with its own tasting and cooking characteristics, and in this book, I will present recipes, techniques, and alternatives to bring out the best in all of them. Because our harvest season is limited—late May through mid-September—most of the summer is spent canning, preserving, and preparing peaches for the freezer. Winter is no excuse for a pieless existence. A delicious peach pie can always be whipped up on demand!

Edgefield County is a long way from the Mississippi Delta where my parents were born, where my grandparents lived, and where I spent some of the best summers of my childhood. I have had the opportunity to visit what used to be the farm twice over the past years, but the farm and house are no longer there—having given way to commercial cotton crops. And although the homestead no longer exists, I will never forget my experiences there. I still stand there, close my eyes and envision a gentler place and time. I can still hear the sounds of farm life and smell the incredible aromas that always flowed from my grandmother's kitchen. In my mind, I can see not only the house, but also the barn, pasture, hen house, pig pen, huge garden with the quince tree in the corner, corn field, smoke house, and yes, even the outhouse! I can see my cousins, brothers, and me playing in the yard and chasing the dog and chickens. But most of all, I can see us on the front porch, in the old rocking chairs, peeling peaches . . .

# History of Peaches

The story of the peach begins in northwest China as far back as 6000 BCE, where it was first domesticated and cultivated. The peach, or *Prunus persica,* is of a deciduous tree, so named because it was very widely cultivated in Persia—modern-day Iran. Belonging to the *Rosaceae* family, same as the plum, apricot, cherry, and almond fruits, peaches are most closely related to nectarines.

Peaches spread to Greece when Alexander the Great conquered the Persians. From there, the ancient Romans spread them throughout Europe. Spanish explorers brought the peach to the Americas in the sixteenth century. With the help of Native American tribes, peach trees spread rapidly throughout the Southeast and were grown in large quantities. By the time the first English settlement arrived on the South Carolina coast in the seventeenth century, peaches were so widely produced that it was thought that they were indigenous to the New World.

In the early eighteenth century, Native American tribes in South Carolina had developed the art of preserving peaches by drying and pressing them into cakes. But it was not until the nineteenth century that commercial peach production began in South Carolina, Georgia, Virginia, Maryland, and Delaware. While peaches are grown in 48 states, they are only commercially produced in 23 states. The top five peach-producing states are California, South Carolina, Georgia, New Jersey, and Pennsylvania.

Today, well over 50 percent of the worlds peaches and nectarines are produced in China, followed by Italy, Spain, the United States, and Greece.

# Interesting Peach Facts

- Peaches are considered a stone fruit, also called a drupe, which means they have a pit inside the flesh that protects the delicate seed.

- Peaches are considered a symbol of good luck, unity, and immortality and were the favored fruit of kings and emperors.

- Brides in China use peach flowers to decorate their hair and wedding bouquets on their wedding day.

- August is National Peach Month in the United States and Canada.

- The peak of peach season is June to August.

- Peaches are the third most popular fruit grown in America.

- After picking, peaches are immediately rinsed in cold water to delay ripening so they don't arrive at market overripe.

- Peaches are defuzzed and sorted by size before sending to market.

- Peaches are packed and shipped in refrigerated trucks, arriving at market three days after picking.

- Flowers appear on the trees before leaves.

- Peaches are always picked from the trees by hand.

- The average life of a peach tree is fifteen years.

- Peach trees produce their best fruit in years four to fifteen.

- The only difference between a peach and a nectarine is that the peach has a fuzzy skin and the nectarine does not.

- Peaches are a great source of vitamin A, B, C, E, and potassium, magnesium, zinc, calcium, sulfur, chlorine, copper, iron, and phosphorous.

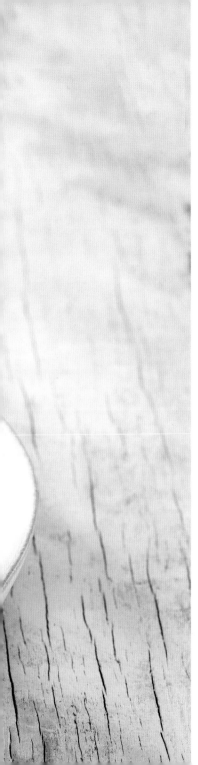

- Peaches are considered a good refresher for the skin because they contain vitamin C, which helps reduce wrinkles and fights skin damage caused by too much exposure to the sun.

- Known as "the fruit of calmness," peaches are said to reduce anxiety.

- Peaches are a good source of fiber, which is good for blood sugar.

- One medium peach contains only 38 calories, and they are naturally fat free.

- There are over 300 varietals of peaches in the United States, and over 2,000 worldwide.

- Peaches used to be known as Persian apples because ancient Romans thought they originated in Persia.

- Peaches are used in the cosmetic and perfume industries for product additives.

- The blood peach, with its red flesh, is indigenous to France's vineyards and is generally only found there.

- The white-fleshed peaches grown in China are sweeter because they have the "honey gene." The yellow-skinned peaches grown in America are more acidic.

- Donut peaches are white-fleshed with velvety skin and a non-clinging pit. Their name is reflective of their shape, which is round and flattened with a dimple in the center. They are also known as Saturn, Jupiter, Chinese, SweetCap, or Saucer peaches. Their candy-sweet and low-acid flavor makes them perfect for eating, canning, desserts, and substituting for regular peaches in most recipes.

- The largest peach cobbler—measuring 11 feet by 5 feet—is made every year in Georgia.

- "You are a peach" is a term that originated from the tradition of giving a peach to someone you like.

Peach
Varietals

# Peach Varietals and Best Uses

The three most common types of peaches grown in the United States are clingstone, semi-freestone and freestone, and among the different types are yellow and white peaches.

Clingstone peaches have flesh that clings to the stone, also referred to as the pit. Semi-freestone peaches have flesh that clings to the pit until it is ripe, and then is fairly easy to remove. Freestone peaches, which are larger and firmer, have flesh that easily separates from the pit. Freestones are less juicy and sweet than clingstones and semi-freestones.

The main difference between yellow and white peaches is the amount of acidity in the peach. Yellow peaches are more acidic and a bit tangy when bitten into. As they ripen, they become sweeter and the background color of the skin turns a deeper yellow. White peaches are less acidic and are sweet, juicy, and will not have that tangy "bite." Unlike yellow peaches, white peaches turn whiter as they ripen.

To properly store peaches at home, place unripe/firm peaches on the counter until they are ripe enough to eat. Once ripe, store in the refrigerator for seven to ten days. Never store an unripe peach in the refrigerator as it will result in a dry, brown, mealy-tasting piece of fruit.

Below is a list of the common peach varietals found in the twenty-three commercially peach-producing states. They are broken down by early-, mid-, and late-season harvests and include stone type and best uses. Harvest times are general and may vary depending on climate and growing zones.

# Peach Varietals

## EARLY-SEASON PEACH VARIETALS

*Harvest: May to June*

*Stone type: Clingstone*

*Best uses: Eating, canning, preserving, desserts*

VARIETAL

Bicentennial
Brittney Lane
Burpeachfourteen
Burpeachnineteen
Burpeachone
Burpeachtwentytwo
Camden
Candor
Carored
Cherry Gold
Correll
Country Sweet
Crimson Lady
Crimson Princess
Delta
Desiree
Derby
Dixired
Earlibelle
Earligrande
Earlired
Empress
Flamin' Fury PF 1
Flamin' Fury PF
    5D Big
Flavorich
Flordabest
Flordacrest
Flordaglobe
Flordaking

Goldcrest
Goldprince
Grezzano
Gulfcrest
Gulfking
Hamlet
Harbelle
June Crest
June Gold
La 120
La Festival
La Percher
Lobo
Manon
Maycrest
May Lady
May Sweet
Nj1350
Queencrest
Regal
Rich Lady
Rich May
Rubired
Rubyprince
Scarletpearl
Sentry
Shepard's Beauty
Sierra Gem
Springbrite
Springcrest
Springold

Springprince
Spring Snow
Starlite
Sugar May
Summerprince
Sunbrite
Super Rich
Surecrop
Suzi Q
Sweethaven
Texstar
UFBeauty
UFGem
UFGlo
UFGold
UFSun
Valleyfire
White Robin
Zee Diamond

## MID-SEASON PEACH VARIETALS

*Harvest: June to July*

*Stone type: Semi-freestone*

*Best uses: Eating, baking, pickling, freezing*

VARIETAL

Allgold
Baby Gold
Bellaire
Brighton
Burpeachfive
Burpeachsix
Carogem
Caroking
Cary Mac
Challenger
Clayton
Comanche
Coronet
CVN #2
Desertred
Diamond Princess
Early Redhaven
Fancy Lady
Fiesta Gem
Fireprince
Flamin' Fury PF 11
    Peach
Flamin' Fury PF 12B
Flamin' Fury
Flamin' Fury PF
    15A
Flamin' Fury PF
    8 Ball
Flamin' Fury PF
    9A-007

Flamin' Fury PF
    Lucky
Flavorcrest
Flordagold
Flordagrande
Flordastar
GaLa
Galactica
Garnet Beauty
Gulfcrimson
Gulfprince
Harbrite
Harken
Harvester
Hawthorne
Idlewild
John Boy
Juneprince
LaGold
LaSweet
Late Sunhaven
LaWhite
Maygold
McNeely
Nectar
Newhaven
Norman
Ranger
Raritan Rose
Red Gold Nectarine
Redhaven
Redtop

Regina
Reliance
Rich Pride
Rio Grande
Rising Star
Saturn
Sentinel
Sierra Rich
Snowbrite
Southern Pearl
Stark EarliGlo
Summer Serenade
Sunfre Nectarine
Sunhaven
Sunland
Sureprince
Suwanee
TexRoyal
Topaz
TropicBeauty
TropicSweet
UFBest
UFOne
UFSharp
Vallegrande
Velvet
Vivid
Washington
White Rock
Wildrose
Zee Pride

## LATE-SEASON PEACH VARIETALS

*Harvest: Mid-June to September*

*Stone type: Freestone*

*Best uses: Pickling, grilling, raw in recipes*

### VARIETAL

| | | | |
|---|---|---|---|
| All Red Elberta | Elegant Lady | Jefferson | September Snow |
| Angelus | Encore | Jerseyglo | September Sun |
| August Lady | Fairtime | Jim Dandee | Snow Giant |
| Augustprince | Fay Elberta | Johnny T | Snow King |
| Autumn Flame | Fayette | Julyprince | Southland |
| Autumnglo | Fire Red | Klondike White | Stagg |
| Autumnprince | Flameprince | La Feliciana | Sugar Giant |
| Baby Gold #7 | Flamin' Fury PF 17 | LaJewel | Sugar Lady |
| Baby Gold #8 | Flamin' Fury PF 20-007 | LaPremier | Sullivan Elberta |
| Belle of Georgia | Flamin' Fury PF 22-007 | Last Chance | Summer Lady |
| Big Red | Flamin' Fury PF 23 | Laurol | Summer Pearl |
| Biscoe | Flamin' Fury PF 24-007 | Legend | Summergold |
| Blake | Flamin' Fury PF 24-C | Loring | Suncrest |
| Blazeprince | Flamin' Fury PF 28-007 | Madison | Sunhigh |
| Bounty | Flamin' Fury PF 35-007 | Majestic | Sunprince |
| Burpeachseven | Flamin' Fury PF Big George | Marqueen | Sweet Dream |
| Burpeachthree | Flamin' Fury PF Lucky 24B | Marsun | Sweet September |
| Calred | Glacier White | Messina | Sweet Sue |
| Canadian Harmony | Glohaven | Milam | Tango |
| Caro Tiger | Golden Glory | Monroe | Tra-Zee |
| Carolina Belle | Glowingstar | O'Henry | Tyler |
| Carolina Gold | Goldilocks | Ouachita Gold | Valley Sweet |
| China Pearl | Gulfsnow | Parade | Venture |
| Contender | Halehaven | Redglobe | White Hale |
| Cresthaven | Harcrest | Redkist | White Lady |
| CVN #4 | Harmony | Redskin | White Princess |
| Denman | Havis | Redsun | White River |
| Dixiland | Honey Dew Hale | Rio Oso Gem | White Rose |
| Early Augustprince | Indian Blood Cling | Ruston Red | White Star |
| Elberta | Intrepid | Ryan Sun | Winblo |
| | J.H. Hale | Sam Houston | Zee Lady |
| | Jayhaven | Scarletprince | |

# Peach Festivals

*L*ooking for a peach festival to attend in your area? The following local peach festivals are held every year throughout the United States and in Canada. While there might not be a festival held in your area, please take advantage of festivals located in cities and states nearest to you.

These peach festivals can range from one day to three days over an extended weekend. At the festivals, you can expect to find lots of peaches and other fruits and vegetables that the participating farmers in the region have to offer. The festivals often feature events like fun parades with vintage cars, cattle and farm animals, contests, and select activities and tours for the child in all of us! Festival organizers have even factored in exciting events to keep the children engaged and entertained, such as animal petting zoos and hay rides. All festivals have activities that are family-fun friendly.

Be prepared to lighten your wallets on the many arts and crafts selections and delicious fair food options available—and whatever you do, don't forget to try the peach ice cream! Finally, when the sun goes down over your wonderfully peachy day, kick back, and enjoy the entertainment and music features offered at many of these festivals.

Exact timing/scheduling may vary for some festivals, so check websites yearly for accurate dates.

## ALABAMA
**Chilton County Peach Festival**
June
Clanton
http://www.
chiltonchamberonline.com

## ARKANSAS
**Annual Johnson County Peach Festival**
June
Clarksville
https://sites.google.com/site/
johnsoncountypeachfestival/

## ARIZONA
**Schnepf Farms Annual Peach Festival**
May
Queen Creek
https://www.schnepffarms.com/
peach-festival/

## CALIFORNIA
**California Peach Festival**
July
Marysville
http://marysvillepeachfest.com

**Live Oak Festival**
September
Live Oak
www.liveoakchamber.org/
peachfestival/

## COLORADO
**Palisade Peach Festival**
August
Palisade
https://palisadepeachfest.com

## DELAWARE
**Fifer's Peach Festival**
August
Wyoming
https://www.fiferorchards.com/
upcoming-events/

**Wyoming Peach Festival**
August
Wyoming
https://wyoming.delaware.gov/
peach-festival/

## GEORGIA
**Georgia Peach Festival**
June
Byron and Fort Valley
http://www.gapeachfestival.com

**Jaemor Farms Peach Festival**
August
Alto
http://www.jaemorfarms.com/
summer-festival

**Morven Peach Festival**
May
Morven
https://festivalnet.com/21271/
Morven-Georgia/Festivals/
Morven-Peach-Festival

## ILLINOIS
**Cobden Peach Festival**
August
Cobden
https://www.enjoyillinois.com/
explore/listing/cobden-peach-
festival

**Grafton Peach Festival**
August
Grafton
http://www.enjoygrafton.com/
events/detail/84/peach-festival-
at-pere-marquette-lodge

## LOUISIANA
**Louisiana Peach Festival**
June
Ruston
https://louisianapeachfestival.org

## MARYLAND
**Leitersburg Peach Festival**
August
Leitersburg
http://www.leitersburgruritan.
org/peach-festival-information.
html.

## MASSACHUSETTS
**Apple-Peach Festival**
September
Acushnet
https://www.
fairhavenneighborhoodnews.
com/apple-peach-
festival-parade/

**Smolak Farm Peach Festival**
August, North Andover
http://www.smolakfarms.com

**Wilbraham Peach Festival**
August
Wilbraham
http://www.peachblossom
festival.org

## MICHIGAN
**Romeo Peach Festival**
September
Romeo
http://romeopeachfestival.com

## MISSOURI
**Missouri Peach Fair**
August
Campbell
http://www.campbellmo.org/
campbell-events

## NEW HAMPSHIRE
**Applecrest Farm Peach Festival**
August
Hampton Falls
http://www.applecrest.com/
festival-schedule.html

## NEW JERSEY
**Community Presbyterian Church Annual Peach Festival**
August
Chester https://cpcchester.org/
peach-festival

**Fine Arts and Peach Festival**
August
Riverton
https://www.riverviewestates.
org/calendar/2017/8/5/fine-arts-
peach-festival

**Gloucester 4-H Fair and Peach Festival**
July
Mullica Hill
https://www.visitnj.org/
nj-events/gloucester-county-
4-h-fair

**Just Peachy Festival**
August
Princeton
https://terhuneorchards.com/
peach-festival/

## NEW YORK
**Annual Peach Festival**
September
Marlboro
http://www.weedorchards.com/
events/

Niagara County Peach
Festival
September
Lewiston
http://lewistonpeachfestival.org

## NORTH CAROLINA
Knotts Island Peach Festival
June
Knotts Island
https://www.everfest.com/e/
knotts-island-peach-festival-
knotts-island-nc

North Carolina Peach
Festival
July
Candor
https://www.ncpeachfestival.
com

## OKLAHOMA
Porter Peach Festival
July
Porter
https://www.porterpeach
festivals.com

Stratford Peach Festival
July
Stratford
http://chickasawcountry.com/
events/stratford-peach-festival

## PENNSYLVANIA
Peach Fest
August
Biglerville
http://hollabaughbros.com/
calendar_events/festivals/

Peach Festival
August
Dillsburg
https://paulusorchards.com/
special-events/

## SOUTH CAROLINA
Lexington County Peach
Festival
July
Gilbert
http://www.
lexingtoncountypeachfestival.
com

McLeod Farms Peach
Festival
July
McBee
https://www.macspride.com

Ridge Peach Festival
June
Trenton
http://www.ridgepeachfestival.
com

South Carolina Peach
Festival
July
Gaffney
https://www.scpeachfest.net

## SOUTH DAKOTA
South Dakota Peach Festival
June
Sioux Falls
http://southdakotapeachfestival.
com/

## TENNESSEE
12 South Farmers Market
Peach Festival
June
Nashville
http://www.12southfarmers
market.com/

Chattanooga Peach Festival
July
Chattanooga
http://chattanoogamarket.com/
peach-festival/

## TEXAS
Charlie Peach Festival
June
Charlie
http://hccchamber.org

Parker County Annual Peach
Festival
July
Weatherford
http://www.
parkercountypeachfestival.org

Stonewall Peach Jamboree
June
Stonewall
https://stonewalltexas.com/
peach-jamboree/

## UTAH
Peach Days
September
Brigham City
https://www.boxelderchamber.
com/peach-days/

## VIRGINIA
Peach Festival
August
Berryville
https://www.
mackintoshfruitfarm.com/
event/peach-festival/

Peach Festival
August
Middletown
http://www.
richardsfruitmarket.com

Virginia State Peach Festival
August
Stuart
https://www.virginia.org/

## WEST VIRGINIA
West Virginia Peach Festival
August
Romney
http://wvpeachfestival.
wordpress.com/event-schedule/

## CANADA
Niagara-On-the-Lake Peach
Festival
August
Niagara-on-the-Lake,
Ontario
https://www.niagaraonthelake.
com/event-calendar

Penticton Peach Festival
August
Penticton, British Columbia
https://peachfest.com

Winona Peach Festival
August
Winona, Ontario
http://winonapeach.com

# Canning & Freezing

# Easy Guide to Canning and Freezing

Peach season is short-lived, and it can be even shorter depending on your location. On average, peach season lasts from late May to mid-September. The easiest way to extend the season—and have this versatile fruit available all year—is to can and freeze peaches while they are abundant and inexpensive. While you can usually find peaches in the supermarkets all year long now, the out-of-season peaches are not nearly as sweet and tasty as peaches that are freshly picked and ripened in season.

If you happen to live or work near a pick-your-own orchard or packing facility, buying in bulk from them will be less expensive than buying peaches at the supermarket. Also, the orchards will likely have "seconds" available for purchase. These are peaches that don't quite meet the strict commercial standards (size and color) of their major supermarket customers but otherwise are perfect for canning, freezing, baking, and eating.

Canning and freezing peaches is not difficult with the proper (inexpensive) equipment. You can master this process in a very short time. Spread out the task over the course of the summer, as the different varieties become available, and you will be able to enjoy your favorite peach dessert when snow is on the ground in the middle of January.

# Substituting Frozen or Canned Peaches

Frozen peaches will produce the same results in baking as fresh peaches. Substitute one-for-one for the recipe amount. There is no need to thaw peaches before baking, especially if they are already sliced. Blind-bake the bottom crust for pies to prevent crust from becoming soggy. Frozen peaches work great in smoothies. If using in salads or other such applications, frozen peaches will need to thaw completely before adding to the dish.

On the other hand, canned peaches are actually cooked as the result of the canning process. First the peaches will need to be drained thoroughly of the juices before using. Second, you will need to increase the amount of canned peaches in adjusting to the recipe. I suggest increasing volume by twenty-five percent (more if needed)—if the recipe call for 4 cups of sliced peaches, use 5 cups. Expect canned peaches to produce a much creamier pie.

# Canning

## EQUIPMENT

7 (1-quart) jars

7 lids and screw bands

21.5-quart water bath canner with insert

Wide-mouth funnel

Large ladle

Canning tongs/jar lifter

## INGREDIENTS

18 pounds peaches

Lemon juice or Fruit-Fresh Produce Protector

5 ½ cups sugar

8 cups water

### SELECT AND PREPARE THE PEACHES

Choose peaches that are firm-ripe—not hard or soft—with no decay, worms, or worm holes and no serious damage, spots, or bruises. If the peaches have only slight damage or imperfections, cut those areas away.

Wash peaches in cold to lukewarm water and peel. (See peeling tip on page 33.)

Cut peaches into halves, quarters, or slices. Discard the pits and peels, or this would be a good time to start a batch of Granddad's Easy Homemade Peach Brandy (page 160).

Sprinkle peaches with lemon juice to keep them from becoming brown or discolored. Stir peaches to make sure all surfaces are covered.

## SANITIZE THE JARS AND LIDS

Sanitize the jars using one of three methods

- wash jars in dishwasher on the sanitize setting
- boil for 10 minutes in water on the stovetop in the canning pot
- heat in a 225-degree-F oven for 20 minutes

To sanitize the lids, place them in a pot of boiling water for 5 minutes.

## PACK FRUIT IN JARS WITH THE "HOT PACK" CANNING METHOD

Hot pack canning is the easiest and preferred method of canning fruit. With this method, the fruit is cooked slightly before packing it in the jars. This removes the air from the fruit, shrinking it and preventing the fruit from floating in the jars. It also extends the shelf life. The sugar mixture helps the fruit to maintain its flavor, bright color, and shape.

In a large Dutch oven, combine the sugar and water. Over medium heat, bring to a boil. Reduce heat to medium-low. Working in batches, put peaches into sugar mixture and cook for 3–4 minutes.

Using the funnel and ladle, fill the jars with peaches and cover with the hot sugar mixture, leaving a ½-inch headspace at the top of each jar.

Wipe jar rims with a clean, damp cloth. Apply lids and rings.

## PROCESS IN A WATER BATH

In a canner prepared with boiling water, submerge the sealed jars, making sure the jars are covered by at least 1 inch of water.

Boil jars for 20–25 minutes.

Using the tongs, remove the jars from the canner and place on a dry, clean towel. Allow to cool overnight.

## CHECK FOR PROPER SEAL AND STORING

After cooling, press down on the center of the lid. If it is concave and does not move up or down when pressed, the jar is sealed. Another test is to remove the ring and see if you can lift the jar by the lid without breaking the seal.

Label all jars with contents and date of canning.

For the jars that did not seal properly, refrigerate and consume first.

Store sealed jars in a cool, dry place.

Canned fruit is best consumed within 1 year.

# Fast, Easy Way to Peel Peaches

When you are canning or doing any preparation that involves peeling lots of peaches, this method is much quicker and easier than using a paring knife—and safer too. This method works for a few or a few bushels of peaches.

Heat water to boiling in a large Dutch oven or saucepan over medium-high heat. Using a paring knife, make an X cut on the bottom of each peach and set aside. In a large aluminum utility bowl, prepare an ice bath.

When the water comes to a boil, working in batches, place peaches in water for 45–60 seconds. Using a slotted spoon, remove peaches, place in ice bath, and allow to cool completely. Where the X was made, you can see the skin pulling away from the peach. Repeat until all peaches are done.

When cool enough to handle, holding peaches in your hand, rub the skin with your fingers to remove the peach skin—it should easily separate from the peach. At this point, continue with your recipe preparation.

# Freezing Peaches

If canning seems a bit time-consuming, but you still want to take advantage of storing peaches for future use, freezing is another option for you.

Line sheet pans (as many as you need to hold your peaches and will fit in your freezer) with parchment paper.

Peel peaches (or not) and slice, quarter, or halve. Sprinkle with freshly squeezed lemon juice.

Spread on the sheet pans. Put in freezer and allow peaches to harden—at least 4 hours or more.

Remove from freezer. Seal peaches in ziplock or vacuum-sealed bags and return to freezer. If you use a ziplock bag, the peaches should be consumed within 1 year. Peaches in vacuum-sealed bags can last up to 3 years.

Recipes

Peaches have customarily been used in desserts or enjoyed as a juicy summer treat. The reality is that the peach is a very versatile fruit, lending itself easily to savory applications, especially when paired with meats like chicken, pork, fish, and lamb. It is not uncommon in Middle Eastern cultures, and indeed cultures around the world, to find peaches applied plentifully to dishes to enhance and awaken the flavors of some of their most revered culinary offerings, such as chutney in India, semifreddo in Portugal, and Kaiserschmarrn in Austria.

As you become more comfortable with the various cooking techniques in this book, it is my hope that you will start to experiment and develop additional uses for peaches in your day-to-day meal preparations.

# Breads & Breakfasts

# Blueberry-Peach-Pecan Scones with Lemon Glaze

*Makes 1 dozen*

2 ¾ cups all-purpose flour

¾ cup sugar

2 teaspoons baking powder

¾ teaspoon baking soda

½ teaspoon salt

½ teaspoon ground cardamom

½ cup (1 stick) butter

½ cup buttermilk or heavy cream

1 large egg

1 lemon, zested

1 teaspoon almond extract

2 medium peaches, peeled and chopped (about 1 cup)

½ cup pecans, toasted and chopped

½ cup frozen blueberries

¼ cup milk, for wash

## LEMON GLAZE

¼ cup freshly squeezed lemon juice

1 cup confectioners' sugar, sifted

*I have always thought of scones as fancy sweet biscuits, and I love them with lots of butter and decadent jams. Traditional scones are plain, but with the addition of peaches, there is no need to add anything else to this delicious treat. These scones are perfect with hot tea in the late afternoon to tide you over until dinner.*

Preheat oven to 400 degrees F.

In a medium bowl, combine the flour, sugar, baking powder, baking soda, salt, and cardamom. Using two knives or a pastry blender, cut in butter until mixture resembles coarse meal. (This step can also be done in the food processor).

Combine the buttermilk, egg, zest, and almond extract. Stir into flour mixture with the peaches, pecans, and blueberries until just combined.

On a lightly floured work surface, use a rolling pin to roll dough to ¾ inch thick. Cut into 4-inch squares using a cookie cutter; then cut each square diagonally, ending with 12 wedges. Place on a parchment-lined baking sheet. Brush with milk and bake for 20–25 minutes, until golden brown.

## LEMON GLAZE

Mix the juice and sugar together in a bowl, stirring until sugar dissolves. If glaze is too thick, add more lemon juice, ½ teaspoon at a time. If too thin, add more sugar, 1 tablespoon at a time, until desired consistency. Drizzle over warm scones.

# Old-Fashioned Tea Cakes
# with Peach-Almond Glaze

*Makes 2 to 3 dozen*
*(depending on size of cookie cutter)*

4 cups all-purpose flour

2 teaspoons baking powder

1 teaspoon ground nutmeg

½ cup buttermilk

1 teaspoon vanilla extract

½ cup light molasses

1 cup (2 sticks) unsalted
butter

1 ½ cups sugar

3 large eggs

PEACH-ALMOND
GLAZE

2 cups confectioners' sugar,
sifted

2 tablespoons peach brandy

½ teaspoon almond extract

*Everyone has childhood memories of something that was just so delicious they have never forgotten about it. For me it was teacakes. My aunt, Lillie B., who lived in Memphis, would always bring them to us when she came to visit. Needless to say, we always looked forward to her visits with great anticipation.*

In a bowl, sift together the flour, baking powder, and nutmeg. Pour the buttermilk into a measuring cup and add the vanilla and molasses to it. In the bowl of a stand mixer, cream together the butter and sugar. Add the eggs, 1 at a time, beating well after each addition. Add the flour mixture, 1 cup at a time, to the butter mixture, alternating with the buttermilk, until a smooth dough forms. (Add additional flour, 1 to 2 tablespoons at a time, if dough is still very sticky.)

On a generously floured surface, knead the dough until soft and smooth. Shape into a disc, wrap with plastic wrap, and refrigerate for 1–2 hours.

Preheat oven to 350 degrees F. Line 2 baking sheets with parchment paper.

Roll out the dough to ½ inch thick. Cut with a cookie cutter, and place tea cakes onto the baking sheets. Bake for 8–10 minutes, until lightly golden brown. Remove the tea cakes from the oven and allow to cool on the pans for 5 minutes. Transfer cakes to a wire rack to cool completely before adding the glaze.

PEACH-ALMOND GLAZE

Place confectioners' sugar into a medium bowl and make a well in the center. Add the brandy and almond extract and stir until thick and smooth. Drizzle or spread over tea cakes. When glaze is set, store in an airtight container for up to 1 week.

# Peach-Pecan Breakfast Muffins

*Makes 12 muffins or 24 mini muffins*

1 ½ cups all-purpose flour

½ cup firmly packed brown sugar

1 ½ teaspoons baking powder

½ teaspoon cinnamon

½ teaspoon kosher salt

1 large egg

¾ cup milk, plus more if needed

½ teaspoon vanilla extract

2 tablespoons honey

5 tablespoons unsalted butter, melted

1 cup peeled and chopped peaches

½ cup chopped pecans

*If you are in a hurry to get out the door in the morning, grab one of these to go. Better yet, put a few in your briefcase or backpack to munch on during the day.*

Preheat oven to 350 degrees F. Line a muffin tin with paper liners.

In a large bowl, whisk together the flour, brown sugar, baking powder, cinnamon, and salt. In a small measuring cup with a spout, combine the egg, milk, vanilla, honey, and butter. Make a well in the middle of the flour mixture and pour in the milk mixture. Stir until just combined. Fold in the peaches and pecans. Batter will be slightly stiff.

Using a scoop or spoon, divide batter evenly among the prepared muffin cups. Bake for 25 minutes, or until a cake tester inserted in the middle of the muffins comes out clean. Serve warm with Honey Butter (page 43) and preserves; or enjoy them as they are.

# Cast Iron Peach Cornbread

*Serves 8*

1 cup cornmeal

1 cup all-purpose flour

½ tablespoon baking powder

½ teaspoon baking soda

¼ cup sugar

½ teaspoon kosher salt

2 large eggs

1 cup buttermilk

4 tablespoons unsalted butter, melted, divided

2 cups chopped unpeeled peaches

Honey Butter, for serving (recipe follows)

*Cornbread is always better when made in a cast iron skillet! Cast iron ensures you get that crispy outer crust time after time. Transport it straight from the oven to the table. For an extra treat, serve it with lots of Honey Butter.*

Preheat oven to 400 degrees F. Put a 9-inch cast iron skillet into the oven.

In a large bowl, mix the cornmeal, flour, baking powder, baking soda, sugar, and salt. In a medium bowl or large measuring cup, combine the eggs, buttermilk, and 2 tablespoons of the butter. Mix the wet ingredients into the dry; do not overmix. Fold the peaches into the batter.

When the oven has reached the desired temperature, carefully remove the skillet and add the remaining butter. Pour the mixture into the skillet and bake for 25–30 minutes, until brown on top. Test the center for doneness. It will be firm to the touch. If brown on top but still soft in the center, cover loosely with aluminum foil, and cook for an additional 5 minutes. Serve with Honey Butter if desired.

# Honey Butter

*Makes approximately 1 cup*

1 cup butter, room temperature

¼ cup honey

Pinch of cinnamon

In a medium bowl, thoroughly combine butter, honey, and cinnamon. Store leftover butter in an airtight container and refrigerate for up to 1 week.

# Buttermilk Peach Waffles

*Makes 6 (8-inch) round waffles*

2 cups all-purpose flour

1 teaspoon baking powder

½ teaspoon baking soda

1 teaspoon kosher salt

3 tablespoons sugar

3 large eggs, beaten

4 tablespoons unsalted butter, melted

2 cups buttermilk, plus more if needed

1 ½ cups finely chopped peaches

*When we were growing up, waffles were always a treat in our house. It took the three of us kids to lift the heavy waffle iron—it seems they weighed a ton back then. My mother would let us make the batter and then look away as we loaded way too much batter onto the iron. My brothers and I thought the batter was supposed to ooze over the sides and spill onto the countertop!*

Preheat waffle iron according to manufacturer's instructions.

In a medium bowl, whisk together the flour, baking powder, baking soda, salt, and sugar. In another medium bowl, beat together the eggs, butter, and milk; then add to dry mixture. Fold in the peaches and let batter rest for 10 minutes.

Spray the waffle iron with nonstick cooking spray. Ladle batter onto the iron. Close top and cook until the waffle is golden brown on both sides. Remove and serve immediately; or keep warm in a 250-degree oven.

# Spinach-Peach Omelet

1 peach, pitted and thinly sliced, plus additional slices for garnish

2 tablespoons sugar

2 tablespoons water

2 large eggs

1 tablespoon milk

1 teaspoon chopped fresh basil

Kosher salt, to taste

Chef Belinda Grains of Paradise or freshly ground black pepper, to taste

1 teaspoon butter or olive oil

¼ cup packed spinach leaves

*Contrary to what you might think, omelets are not difficult to make. By following the easy steps below, the omelet just went from a fancy Sunday brunch kind of an event to an everyday possibility. You could easily substitute canned peaches in this recipe and eliminate the step of having to cook the peaches first.*

In a saucepan over medium-low heat, cook the peaches, sugar, and water until peaches are soft but not falling apart. Drain and set aside.

In a medium bowl, whisk together the eggs, milk, and basil; season with the salt and spice blend.

In an 8-inch omelet pan over medium heat, add the butter. Add egg mixture and reduce temperature to medium low. Let eggs cook for about 30 seconds until just starting to set. With a heat-resistant spatula, lift the sides of the omelet and tilt the pan to let uncooked eggs run under the omelet. Do this all the way around the omelet until it is set (no longer runny). Spread the spinach on one side of the omelet and place the sliced peach on top of the spinach. Using the spatula, fold the other side of the omelet over onto the peach slices. Transfer to a plate and serve. Garnish with additional peach slices.

# Hot Curried Peaches

6 medium peaches, peeled and sliced

1 cup dried cherries or cranberries

5 tablespoons unsalted butter

½ cup firmly packed light brown sugar

2 teaspoons curry powder

1 ½ teaspoons Chef Belinda Moroccan Blend or cinnamon

Pinch of kosher salt

*This versatile recipe is an adaptation of one I received from my good friend Kathy Huff Cunningham. It works for breakfast served over pancakes or for dessert atop a big scoop of vanilla ice cream or a slice of pound cake. You can even serve it as a side with grilled pork chops or chicken. Canned or frozen peaches can easily be used if fresh are not available.*

Preheat oven to 325 degrees F.

Place peaches and cherries in a 9 x 9-inch baking dish. In a small saucepan over medium-low heat (or in the microwave), melt the butter. Remove from heat and stir in the brown sugar, curry powder, spice blend, and salt. Spoon over the peaches and cherries. Bake for 45 minutes to 1 hour, until peaches are soft and syrupy.

To make ahead, cover and store in the refrigerator. Reheat in 350-degree oven for 30 minutes.

# Appetizers

# Mascarpone Prosciutto Peach Crostini

*Makes 12*

1 large firm peach, cut into 12 thick slices

Olive oil spray

½ cup balsamic vinegar

12 crostini (recipe follows)

4 ounces mascarpone

Arugula

6 slices prosciutto, halved

## CROSTINI

1 baguette, diagonally sliced

Olive oil spray

*What I like about this appetizer is its versatility: make it with grilled peaches or plain, crostini or just sliced baguette, prosciutto or not, or drizzled with reduced balsamic or honey. This is the peach appetizer of endless possibilities.*

Spray peaches with olive oil. On a grill pan or outdoor grill at medium heat, place peach slices crosswise so they don't fall through the grates. Grill for 2–3 minutes on each side until you see grill marks. Do not allow to get too soft. Remove from grill.

In a small saucepan over medium-high heat, bring the vinegar to a boil. Reduce to a simmer and let cook until reduced by half. Remove from heat and let cool.

Place crostini on a large serving platter. Spread each slice with mascarpone. Top each with arugula, a piece of prosciutto, and a peach slice. When ready to serve, drizzle with the balsamic reduction. Transfer any leftover reduction to a small jar and refrigerate.

## CROSTINI

Preheat oven to 350 degrees F. Spray each slice with olive oil on both sides. Place on a sheet pan and bake for 15–20 minutes, until slightly golden. Cool on pan. Store in a ziplock bag if not using immediately.

# Brie-Peach Beggar's Purse

*Makes 32*

32 dumpling or wonton
    wrappers

1 (8-ounce) wheel Brie

2 peaches, peeled and diced
    into ½-inch pieces

Safflower or sunflower oil,
    for frying

*I was first introduced to this concept as a part of the cheese and dessert course in a Saumur, France, restaurant. It was initially presented as a slice of Camembert baked in a crepe. There was an immediate connection there for me, but I savored it more as an appetizer. At the time, I was working on this cookbook and it struck me that adding a bit of peach would enhance the overall flavor profile and make for a simple, delicious hors d'oeuvre.*

Lay the wrappers on a clean, dry surface. Slice the Brie into quarters. Cut each quarter into 4 slices; then cut each slice in half. You should end up with 32 pieces of cheese. If not prepping immediately, chill the cheese so pieces do not become warm and stick together.

Place 1 piece of Brie onto each wrapper and top with a cube of peach. Using your finger or a small pastry brush, brush the ends of the wrappers with water—just enough to moisten, not saturate. Bring opposite pointed ends together and press to seal about halfway down. Then bring the other opposite ends together and press to seal completely. Twist the top slightly to give a decorative touch. Place on a large platter and repeat the process until all wrappers, cheese, and peaches are used. Place in the refrigerator for 30 minutes.

In a deep skillet or Dutch oven, heat 3–4 inches of oil over medium-high heat. Fry purses, 4–5 at a time, for 3–4 minutes, until they turn golden brown and rise to the top of the oil. Drain on paper towels. Serve warm or room temperature.

# Peach Guacamole

2 ripe avocados

1 large peach, peeled and chopped

1 jalapeño, seeded and finely chopped

2 tablespoons chopped red onion

2 tablespoons chopped fresh cilantro

Juice of 1 lime

Kosher salt, to taste

Freshly ground black pepper, to taste

*Guacamole is a crowd pleaser anytime, anywhere. Add the sweetness of a peach and the entire flavor profile changes. Snack on it with some chips, dollop it on your tacos, or spread it on your hamburger. The beauty is that you don't have to wait for summer to enjoy this, because it's just as easily made with frozen peaches.*

Halve the avocados and remove the pit. Using a spoon, scoop the flesh into a medium-size bowl. Then coarsely smash with a potato masher. Add the peach, jalapeño, onion, cilantro, and lime juice; season with salt and pepper. Thoroughly mix all of the ingredients together. Transfer to a serving bowl and serve immediately. If not serving immediately, cover with plastic wrap, pressing the wrap onto the surface of the guacamole to prevent it from turning brown. Refrigerate until served.

# Crab Cakes with Peach-Jalapeño Salsa

*Makes 8*

## CRAB CAKES

1 tablespoon unsalted butter

2 tablespoons olive oil, plus more for frying

¾ cup sliced green onions

1 clove garlic, minced

1 pound lump crabmeat, picked over to remove any shell

1 ½ cups breadcrumbs, divided

⅓ cup heavy cream

1 large egg

2 tablespoons freshly squeezed lemon juice

1 tablespoon Dijon mustard

½ teaspoon Peri Peri Spice Mix (see facing page)

¼ cup chopped fresh parsley

Lemon wedges, for garnish

*This recipe is inspired by my good friend Geeta Narian, with whom I had the pleasure of sharing many a meal during my three years living in Johannesburg, South Africa. There, you'll find a rich history of South African, Afrikaans, and Indian food. This is her Indian family's fish cake recipe that I easily adapted for crab cakes. It uses peri peri, which can refer to either the blazing-hot African bird's eye chile or a complex spice blend popular in South Africa. The crab cakes use the spice blend, not the pepper that registers 175,000 on the Scoville scale. Try the spice blend on chicken and pork too—think of it as South Africa's rendition of jerk seasoning. I peel the jalapeños for the salsa, which I often do for dishes that are not cooked.*

## CRAB CAKES

In a large skillet over medium heat, melt the butter and oil. Sauté the onions for 3–4 minutes, and then add the garlic. Sauté for an additional minute until onions are soft. Set aside to cool.

Gently mix together the cooled onions (setting the skillet aside for later use), crabmeat, ½ cup of the breadcrumbs, cream, egg, lemon juice, mustard, spice mix, and parsley. Cover and chill for 30 minutes.

Shape the crab mixture into 8 (3-inch) cakes and coat with the remaining breadcrumbs.

Heat 2–3 tablespoons olive oil in the reserved skillet over medium heat. Cook the crab cakes for 4–5 minutes on each side, until golden brown. Drain on paper towels and keep in a warm oven until ready to serve. Serve with the Peach-Jalapeño Salsa.

## PEACH-JALAPEÑO SALSA

2 peaches, peeled and diced, divided

1 jalapeño, peeled, if desired, and finely diced

¼ cup freshly squeezed lime juice

2 tablespoons finely chopped fresh cilantro

¼ cup honey

1 tablespoon finely chopped red onion

## PERI PERI SPICE MIX

1 teaspoon ground cayenne pepper

½ teaspoon crushed red pepper flakes

2 teaspoons paprika

1 teaspoon onion powder

1 teaspoon garlic powder

½ teaspoon ground ginger

½ teaspoon ground cinnamon

½ teaspoon kosher salt

½ teaspoon dried lemon peel

1 teaspoon dried oregano

## PEACH-JALAPEÑO SALSA

In the bowl of a food processor, combine half the peaches and the remaining salsa ingredients. Pulse until smooth. Stir in the remaining peaches and chill until ready to serve.

## PERI PERI SPICE MIX

Mix all ingredients together and store in a glass jar.

# Prosciutto-Wrapped Peaches with Balsamic Reduction

*Makes 8*

1 cup balsamic vinegar

2 medium peaches, peeled and quartered

4 slices prosciutto, halved lengthwise

Fresh mint leaves, for garnish

*The fresh peaches, salty prosciutto, and sweet balsamic vinegar create a perfect appetizer or first course. They hold up for quite a long time, so feel free to make them on the morning of an evening get-together. These little fruit wraps also pack easily into a lunch box and offer a healthy pick-me-up when you feel the urge to snack between meals.*

In a small pan, bring the vinegar to a boil over medium-high heat. Reduce heat to medium-low and simmer for about 10 minutes, until the vinegar coats the back of a spoon. Remove from heat and let cool before serving. If not using immediately, store in an airtight bottle. This reduction keeps in the refrigerator for a few months.

Wrap each peach quarter with a slice of prosciutto, drizzle with balsamic reduction, and garnish with mint.

# Peachy Ham-Gruyère Panini

*Makes 16 appetizers;*
*or serves 4 as an entrée*

8 slices ciabatta bread, divided

¼ cup Dijon mustard

8 thin slices Black Forest ham

8 thin slices Gruyère cheese

12 thin slices dill pickle, plus more for serving

1 large peach, cut into 12 slices

Arugula or baby spinach

¼ cup unsalted butter, softened

*This is the ultimate modern picnic sammie. Use ciabatta, French or Italian loaf, sourdough, or Cuban bread. It's good any way you slice it! Cut it into smaller pieces as an appetizer or eat it whole as a meal with a small green salad. For breakfast you can serve this sandwich with a poached egg on top, smothered in hollandaise sauce. This is as good and versatile a sandwich as you'll ever get anywhere.*

Heat a panini grill to medium heat. Spread the bread slices with mustard and arrange mustard side up. Top 4 slices of bread with 2 slices ham, 2 slices cheese, 3 slices pickles, and 3 slices peaches. Cover with arugula and top with the remaining 4 slices of bread.

Spread the outside of the sandwiches with butter on both sides; place on the grill. Lower the top of the grill. Cook until the cheese starts to melt and grill marks form on the bread. Remove from the grill and let rest for 5 minutes before serving. Serve with additional pickles; or slice each panini into 4 equal pieces and pass as appetizers.

# Soups, Salads & Sides

# Peach and Tomato Gazpacho

*Serves 4 To 6*

6 ripe peaches, quartered

6 ripe tomatoes, quartered

2 shallots, peeled and halved

1 clove garlic, peeled

1 stalk celery with leaves

2 to 3 tablespoons extra virgin olive oil, plus more for topping

Juice of 1 lime (about 2 tablespoons)

1 ½ tablespoons chopped fresh tarragon

Kosher salt, to taste

Pinch of cayenne, or more to taste

Seasoned pepitas, for garnish

Lime wedges, for garnish

*No longer will those overripe tomatoes and peaches go to waste. Repurpose them into this cold and refreshing soup for lunchtime or as a starter for your alfresco meal. Gazpacho may be easy to prepare, but don't underestimate the layers of flavors that abound here. From the sweetness of the ripe peaches and tomatoes to the slight bitterness of the tarragon, both are enriched with the addition of lime juice. Refrigerating overnight only improves the flavor. Serve as it comes from the blender or strain for a silkier texture.*

In a blender, purée the peaches, tomatoes, shallots, garlic, and celery until smooth. Add the oil, lime juice, tarragon, salt, and cayenne; continue blending until all ingredients are combined. Pour into a carafe or pitcher with a lid and refrigerate. If desired, strain through a fine sieve before refrigeration.

To serve, ladle into bowls or cups and garnish with pepitas and lime, and drizzle with a little more olive oil.

# Chilled Peach-Mint Soup

3 large peaches, peeled, halved, and pitted

2 tablespoons firmly packed brown sugar

1 ½ tablespoons honey

1 ½ cups freshly squeezed orange juice

½ teaspoon ground cardamom

¼ teaspoon sea salt

2 teaspoons crème de menthe

¼ cup sour cream

½ vanilla bean, split lengthwise and seeds scraped

Mint sprigs, for garnish

Peach slices, for garnish

*This sweet soup is a summer picnic's dream—just transport in a thermos and serve in demitasse cups or shot glasses. Even with the sugar, the soup reads more savory, getting earthy undertones from the cardamom.*

Preheat oven to 375 degrees F. Line a shallow, rimmed baking sheet with parchment paper.

In a large bowl, toss the peaches, brown sugar, and honey. Place peaches, cut side down, on the prepared baking sheet. Roast for 15 minutes; turn over, and continue roasting until tender and juices begin to caramelize, about 10 minutes.

Scrape peaches and pan juices into a food processor and let cool. Add the orange juice, cardamom, salt, and crème de menthe; process until smooth. Transfer soup to a medium bowl. Cover and refrigerate until cold.

In small bowl, mix the sour cream and the vanilla bean seeds. Ladle soup into 4 bowls; top with a dollop of vanilla-flavored sour cream. Garnish each with a mint sprig and fresh peach slice, if desired.

# Peach-Pistachio Chicken Salad

½ cup extra virgin olive oil

¼ cup red wine vinegar

1 tablespoon freshly squeezed lemon juice

½ teaspoon kosher salt

¼ teaspoon freshly ground black pepper

2 peaches, quartered

6 cups arugula

¼ red onion, sliced

1 stalk celery, thinly sliced diagonally

2 cups shredded cooked chicken

½ cup crumbled feta cheese

½ cup pistachios

*This recipe makes great use of grocery store rotisserie chicken and offers a twist on the more expected chicken salad with grapes and almonds. I call for grilling the peaches because it intensifies the flavors—and it looks pretty, too. But it's not necessary if you're short on time.*

Whisk the oil, vinegar, lemon juice, salt, and pepper in a small bowl until emulsified. Brush the peaches with oil. In a grill pan on the stovetop, or over a hot outdoor grill, grill peaches on the flesh surfaces until grill marks form, 4–5 minutes. Let cool and then slice.

In a large salad bowl, toss the arugula, onion, and celery with a little bit of the vinaigrette. Arrange the chicken, peaches, and cheese atop the dressed greens and sprinkle with more of the vinaigrette. Top with the pistachios.

# Spinach-Peach Salad with Stilton Cheese and Walnuts

*Serves 4*

½ tablespoon butter

1 small red onion, peeled, halved, and sliced

½ cup walnut halves

4 peaches, quartered

Canola oil, for brushing

6 cups baby spinach

Kosher salt and freshly ground black pepper, to taste

Peach Vinaigrette (page 151)

½ cup crumbled Stilton cheese

*This salad just screams summer. The combined taste of caramelized onions, peaches, and Stilton cheese is amazing. And when paired with the Peach Vinaigrette, this salad is a keeper. If you can't find Stilton easily, substitute another variety of blue cheese like Gorgonzola, Roquefort, or Danish Blue.*

In a large sauté pan over medium-high heat, melt the butter. Add the onion and spread out in the pan. Cook, stirring only occasionally, for about 30 minutes, or until brown. Set aside.

In a dry sauté pan over medium heat, toast the walnuts for about 2 minutes, until they smell toasty and appear darker in color.

Brush the peaches with oil. In a grill pan on the stovetop, or over a hot outdoor grill, grill peaches on the flesh surfaces until grill marks form, 4–5 minutes. Allow peaches to slightly cool then slice.

Arrange the spinach in a large salad bowl or platter; sprinkle with onions, peaches, and walnuts. Season with salt and pepper. Drizzle with a few tablespoons of the vinaigrette and toss lightly. Add the cheese and serve.

# Peach-Avocado Pasta Salad

8 ounces ditalini pasta, or other small pasta shapes

¼ cup extra virgin olive oil

3 tablespoons blood orange vinegar

1 tablespoon chopped fresh basil

Kosher salt and freshly ground black pepper, to taste

2 ears corn, cooked and kernels cut off the cob

2 Haas avocados, sliced and tossed with lemon juice

2 large peaches, quartered or sliced and tossed with lemon juice

*This sweet-meets-savory pasta salad makes a good side when serving an outdoor meal. Nothing here to spoil if left out while you enjoy your meal and guests.*

Cook the pasta according to package instructions. Meanwhile, in a measuring cup with a spout, blend the oil, vinegar, basil, salt, and pepper. Drain and cool the pasta. If pasta starts to get dry, toss with a tablespoon of dressing.

Transfer pasta to a large serving bowl or platter. Place the corn, avocados, and peaches on top of pasta; toss lightly with dressing. Refrigerate if not serving immediately.

# Tropical Peach-Berry Salad

2 peaches, sliced

1 pint strawberries, hulled and halved

1 cup blackberries

½ pineapple, peeled, cored, and sliced

2 kiwis, peeled and sliced

4 ounces vanilla yogurt

2 tablespoons freshly squeezed lime juice

2 tablespoons honey

Mint leaves, for garnish

*This fruit salad is a refreshing snack any time of the day. Eat it alone without dressing or over plain Greek yogurt. Serve it over sorbet for dessert.*

Arrange the fruit on a large serving platter. In a medium bowl, combine the yogurt, lime juice, and honey. Drizzle fruit lightly with dressing. Garnish with mint leaves. Refrigerate if not serving immediately.

# Simple Peach Garden Salad
# with Peach Vinaigrette

8 cups baby summer lettuce
  greens, escarole, or frisée

1 Belgian endive, cut
  diagonally

½ red onion, sliced

2 large ripe peaches, each cut
  into 8 wedges

½ cup toasted pine nuts,
  divided

½ cup Peach Vinaigrette
  (page 151)

*Last-minute guests? Serve this salad up with an easy roasted chicken in one hour or less— especially if you get a fully-cooked rotisserie chicken at the supermarket.*

Rinse the lettuce and arrange on a salad platter or bowl. Add the endive, onion, peaches, and ¼ cup of the pine nuts; lightly toss with vinaigrette.

Sprinkle the remaining pine nuts on top.

# Peach-Sweet Potato Casserole

*Serves 6 to 8*

*This savory dish could almost pass for dessert. Creamy, spiced sweet potatoes get a hit of bourbon and a decadent pecan streusel topping. Serve it as a side to pork, lamb, or turkey—it steals the show every time. Use fresh ripe peaches or peaches you've canned.*

## TOPPING

1 cup firmly packed light brown sugar

⅓ cup flour

4 tablespoons butter, softened

½ cup chopped pecans

## CASSEROLE

4 large or 6 medium sweet potatoes, baked and cooled

4 tablespoons butter

½ cup firmly packed light brown sugar

¼ teaspoon nutmeg

1 teaspoon vanilla extract

⅓ cup heavy cream

2 tablespoons bourbon

2 to 3 cups ripe peeled peach slices

Preheat oven to 350 degrees F. Grease a 9 x 13-inch baking dish.

## TOPPING

In a small bowl, combine the brown sugar, flour, and butter with a fork until crumbly. Stir in the pecans and set aside.

## CASSEROLE

Peel the sweet potatoes, discard the skins, and place the flesh in the bowl of a stand mixer. Add the butter, brown sugar, nutmeg, and vanilla; beat until thoroughly combined. Add the cream and bourbon and continue beating until smooth.

Pour half of the mixture into the prepared baking dish. Cover with sliced peaches and finish with remaining sweet potato mixture. Top with the brown sugar topping. Bake, uncovered, for 30 minutes, or until top is golden brown.

To make ahead, prepare the casserole, but do not bake. Cover with plastic wrap, and then cover with aluminum foil and freeze. When ready to bake, thaw in the refrigerator overnight. Uncover and bake at 350 degrees F, increasing baking time to 45 minutes or slightly longer.

# Main Courses

# Peach-Glazed Ham Steak

*Serves 4*

2 peaches, peeled and chopped small

2 tablespoons firmly packed brown sugar

2 tablespoons water

1 teaspoon ancho chile powder

1 teaspoon Dijon mustard

½ teaspoon ground cardamom

1 smoked ham steak, ½-inch thick (about 1 ¼ pound)

*Ham steak is traditionally thought of as a breakfast item, but properly prepared, it can be an anytime-of-the-day meal. Feeding a crowd? Use this glaze recipe on a whole ham—just double the glaze ingredients.*

In a small saucepan over medium-low heat, combine the peaches, brown sugar, water, chile powder, mustard, and cardamom. Cook, stirring occasionally, until thickened and peaches start to break down, about 20 minutes.

Make diagonal cuts, 1 inch apart, into outer edges of ham steak to prevent it from curling up on the grill. On an outdoor grill or an indoor grill pan, over medium-high heat, place the ham steak and brush the top with glaze. Cook for 4–5 minutes and turn over. Brush the cooked side with glaze and cook for another 4–5 minutes. Remove to a platter, brush once more with the glaze, and let rest for 5 minutes.

# Blackened Cod Tacos with Peach Salsa

*Serves 4*

2 pounds cod fillets, cut into 8 strips

Chef Belinda Blackened Spice Blend, or a Mexican spice blend or taco seasoning, to taste

Extra virgin olive oil

8 soft corn tortillas

2 cups shredded red cabbage

Peach Salsa (page 141), to taste

½ cup pickled jalapeño slices

2 avocados, each cut into 8 slices and tossed with lemon juice

Lime wedges, for serving

*Whether celebrating Cinco de Mayo, tailgating at a sports event, or just in the mood for Mexican fare, these tacos are easy, filling, and—with the blackened seasoning—pack in a lot of flavor. Pair these with a pitcher of Peach Margaritas (page 162), and let the fun begin!*

Season the cod on both sides with the spice blend and sprinkle with oil. Cook on a stovetop grill pan over medium heat for 2–3 minutes each side until opaque.

Warm the tortillas, 1 at a time, in a dry cast iron skillet over medium-high heat for 20–25 seconds per side, until they smell toasty and start to get dark spots. Keep warm in a tortilla holder or dish covered with a kitchen towel.

To assemble, divide the cabbage, cod, salsa, jalapeños, and avocado slices evenly among the warm tortillas. Serve with lime wedges.

# Prawn, Peach, and Pineapple Kebabs with Spicy Peach-Jalapeño Salsa

¼ cup chili oil

2 tablespoons freshly squeezed lime juice

2 to 3 scallions, cut into 1-inch diagonal slices

2 pounds (U/15) prawns (24 large prawns or shrimp), shelled and deveined with tails on

8 (12-inch) skewers

6 small peaches, quartered

24 (1 ½-inch) pineapple chunks

Spicy Peach-Jalapeño Salsa (page 142), for serving

Lime wedges, for serving

*Kebabs are a great outdoor entertaining option. Easy to cook and eat, the kebabs can be assembled ahead of time and grilled at your convenience. Use 6-inch skewers for appetizer-size kebabs.*

In a large non-reactive bowl or ziplock bag, combine the chili oil, lime juice, scallions, and prawns. Make sure all prawns are covered with marinade. Refrigerate for 30–45 minutes. If using wooden skewers, soak them in water for 30 minutes.

Preheat grill to medium, 350 degrees F.

Alternate 3 prawns, 3 peach quarters and 3 pineapple chunks onto each skewer. Grill over direct heat for about 4 minutes on each side until prawns are opaque. Remove from grill and serve with salsa and lime wedges.

# Thyme-Peach Chicken Breasts

*Serves 4*

4 bone-in chicken breasts

Chef Belinda Everyday Spice Blend or all-purpose seasoning, to taste

Extra virgin olive oil

4 to 5 shallots, peeled

4 cloves garlic, peeled

4 peaches, unpeeled and quartered

Handful of thyme sprigs

¼ cup white wine

*When I cook chicken breasts, I prefer the bone-in breasts. I think you will find that they have more flavor, as does any meat cooked on the bone. And the bone-in breast will be juicier. After baking, you can remove the bone if you prefer. I always leave it, because I think it adds to the presentation, especially if served in a rustic dish or a cast iron skillet. No need to worry about preparing an extra sauce for this dish. As the chicken bakes, it will naturally form its own sauce with the help of the other ingredients in the pan. It doesn't get any easier than this!*

Preheat oven to 350 degrees F.

Rinse and pat dry the chicken. Season on both sides with spice blend and place in a baking dish. Sprinkle all over with oil. Spread the shallots, garlic, peaches, and thyme all around chicken and add the wine. Bake for 45–60 minutes, depending on size of breasts, until temperature reaches 165 degrees F on an instant-read thermometer.

# Greek-Style Beef Stew with Peaches

*Serves 6 to 8*

3 pounds boneless chuck, eye of round, or rump roast, cut into 2-inch chunks

Kosher salt and freshly ground black pepper, to taste

4 tablespoons extra virgin olive oil, divided

2 onions, chopped

3 carrots, thick-sliced diagonally

3 stalks celery, thick-sliced diagonally

4 to 5 cloves garlic, peeled and smashed

2 tablespoons all-purpose flour

1 (750 ml) bottle red wine, or 3 cups beef stock, plus more as needed

2 tablespoons tomato paste

2 bay leaves

3 oregano sprigs

1 rosemary sprig

3 whole cloves

6 peaches, each cut into 8 slices

*This braised beef dish is reminiscent of a very popular Greek beef stew called stifado. Greek and Middle Eastern stews and meat dishes often include warming spices such as nutmeg, allspice, and cloves, which result in unique flavor profiles. Here, the cloves unwrap the peach's natural sweetness. If the wine is too bold for your taste, use beef stock or a combination of both.*

Preheat oven to 350 degrees F.

Season the beef with salt and pepper. In a large Dutch oven over medium-high heat, heat 2 tablespoons of the oil. Working in batches, brown beef on all sides and remove to a platter. Add the remaining oil to pan, reduce heat to medium, and sauté the onions and carrots until onions are translucent. Add the celery and garlic and sauté 1 minute longer. Sprinkle the flour over vegetable mixture and stir.

Carefully pour the wine into the Dutch oven and stir well, scraping up any bits on the bottom. Return beef to the pot, add tomato paste, and stir until well-mixed. Tie bay leaves, oregano, rosemary, and cloves in a large piece of cheesecloth with a long piece of kitchen twine. Attach the herb packet to the handle of the Dutch oven with the loose end of the twine; then place the packet into the stew mixture. Bring to a boil. Cover and place in oven and cook for 2 hours. Add the peaches and cook for an additional 30 minutes, or until beef is fork-tender. If mixture appears to be getting a little dry or too thick, add an additional cup of wine (or beef stock).

# Herb-Crusted Peach Mustard Pork Tenderloin

Serves 4

1 (1 ¼-pounds) pork tenderloin

Kosher salt and freshly ground black pepper

1 tablespoon extra virgin olive oil

3 to 4 tablespoons Peach Mustard (page 144), plus additional for serving

1 tablespoon chopped fresh rosemary

1 tablespoon chopped fresh thyme

1 tablespoon chopped fresh sage

¼ cup white wine

*Pork tenderloin is a favorite at our house for entertaining. This wonderfully tender cut of pork is delicious with minimal seasoning, and it is also a blank canvas for bold and sweet flavors. This peach mustard is just the thing to bring to life its many subtle characteristics.*

Preheat oven to 350 degrees F.

Season the tenderloin with salt and pepper. Heat oil in a large ovenproof skillet over medium-high heat. Brown tenderloin on all sides and remove from heat. Using a pastry brush, brush mustard over all sides of tenderloin.

In a small bowl, mix together the rosemary, thyme, and sage; sprinkle herbs on all sides of tenderloin, patting to adhere to meat. Return tenderloin to skillet and add the wine. Put in the oven and bake for 25–35 minutes, until the temperature on an instant-read thermometer reaches 145 degrees F. Remove from oven and let rest for 15 minutes. Slice and serve with additional mustard.

# Peach Bourbon-Roasted Chicken

*Serves 4*

1 (3 to 4 pound) chicken

Chef Belinda Everyday Spice
Blend, or all-purpose
seasoning, to taste

½ onion, halved

5 to 6 cloves garlic, peeled

½ lemon, halved

6 to 7 sprigs oregano

1 cup Savory Bourbon Peach
Sauce (page 145)

2 peaches, peeled and
quartered

*The star of the family Sunday dinner! The addition of the peach bourbon glaze adds moisture and complexity to this all-time favorite entrée. As the bourbon in the sauce cooks down, the remaining mixture will thicken to a syrupy consistency, leaving just a hint of alcohol. Used to baste the chicken as it cooks, the glaze acts as a tenderizer, and the result is a glistening, gorgeous mahogany bird.*

Place a cast iron skillet into the oven and heat oven to 500 degrees F.

Rinse and pat dry the chicken. Season chicken inside and out with the spice blend. Place the onion, garlic, lemon, and oregano into the cavity. Truss the legs and fold wings under chicken.

Divide the bourbon sauce between two small bowls; reserve one bowl to serve with chicken.

Remove hot skillet from the oven and transfer chicken to the skillet. Brush the chicken with half the sauce. Return the skillet to the oven and cook for 15 minutes; then lower the temperature to 350 degrees F. Spread the peaches around the chicken and cook for an additional 40–45 minutes, basting occasionally with additional sauce, until the temperature reaches 165 degrees F on an instant-read thermometer. If the chicken is getting too brown, cover loosely with aluminum foil.

Remove from the oven and let rest for 15 minutes before serving. Cut into desired pieces and serve with the reserved sauce and cooked peaches.

# Berbere Flat Iron Steak with Honey Grilled Peaches

*Berbere is a spice blend used in North African cooking, particularly in Ethiopia, and this well-balanced combination of sweet and savory flavors complements grilled meats and stews. Here, it's used in combination with peaches, which come to life with the warmth of the nutmeg, ginger, and cloves in the berbere. Feel free to double or quadruple the spice blend and save the rest for another roasted meat.*

### BERBERE

2 tablespoons paprika

1 tablespoon ancho chile powder

1 teaspoon ground coriander

1 teaspoon turmeric

½ teaspoon kosher salt

½ teaspoon fenugreek powder

¼ teaspoon ground nutmeg

¼ teaspoon ground ginger

¼ teaspoon ground allspice

¼ teaspoon ground cloves

### STEAK

2 flat iron steaks

Extra virgin olive oil

2 large peaches, halved and pitted

1 tablespoon honey

### BERBERE

In a small bowl, mix together the paprika, chile powder, coriander, turmeric, salt, fenugreek, nutmeg, ginger, allspice, and cloves.

### STEAK

Rub berbere generously onto both sides of steak and wrap in plastic wrap. Store in the refrigerator overnight. Remove from refrigerator 30 minutes before grilling

Preheat grill to medium-high. Sprinkle steak on both sides with oil. Grill for 4–5 minutes on each side, or to desired doneness. (Temperature for rare is 130–135 degrees F, medium-rare is 140 degrees F, medium is 155 degrees F, and well-done is 165 degrees F.) Remove from grill and cover with foil. Remember, steak will continue to cook after removed from grill; you may want to shave a few minutes off the cooking time to prevent overcooking. Keep the grill heated.

While steak is resting, brush peach halves with oil; grill for about 8 minutes, turning once, until charred and tender. Remove peaches from grill, cut into wedges, and drizzle with honey. Cut steak into thin slices—cutting across the grain—and serve with the peach wedges.

# Grilled Fish with Peach-Pepper Relish

*Serves 4*

4 teaspoons freshly squeezed lemon juice

4 teaspoons extra virgin olive oil

½ teaspoon paprika

1 clove garlic, minced

4 (6-ounce) skinless fish fillets, of choice

Chef Belinda Seafood Spice Blend or salt and freshly ground black pepper, to taste

Nonstick cooking spray

Peach-Pepper Relish (page 149), for serving

*This is a gem of a recipe for summertime entertaining that you will use over and over again. Quick and easy, it will work with any firm, thick fish like cod, salmon, halibut, or bass. Give it a try with chicken, too!*

In a large, shallow glass baking dish, combine the lemon juice, oil, paprika, and garlic. Add the fish and turn to coat. Cover and allow to marinate for 15 minutes.

Heat outdoor grill or grill pan to medium-high. Remove fish from the marinade and discard marinade. Sprinkle fish with spice blend. Coat the preheated grill or grill pan with cooking spray. Grill fish for 3 minutes on each side, or to desired degree of doneness. Serve with the relish.

# Peach-Stuffed Pork Chops

4 (1 ½-inch-thick) rib pork chops, Frenched (meat scraped from the lower bone)

Chef Belinda Everyday Spice Blend, or all-purpose seasoning, to taste

4 tablespoons extra virgin olive oil, divided

1 cup diced sweet onions

1 ½ cup diced peaches

⅓ cup all-purpose flour

1 cup white wine, plus more as needed

¼ cup firmly packed brown sugar

1 teaspoon cinnamon

2 cups peeled and sliced peaches

*My inspiration for this recipe is my longtime hometown of Trenton, South Carolina, in Edgefield County—the peach capital of the South, and the second largest peach producing area in the United States. Every year on the third Saturday of June, the Ridge Peach Festival is held here. We are serious about our peaches!*

Preheat oven to 350 degrees F. Cut a pocket into each pork chop, with a 1 ½-inch opening for stuffing. Your butcher can do this for you.

Season chops inside and out with spice blend. Warm a large ovenproof skillet over medium-high heat and add 2 tablespoons of the oil. Sauté the onions until soft and translucent. Remove and cool slightly. Mix the onions with the diced peaches and stuff into chops. Secure the openings with toothpicks, if necessary, to prevent stuffing from coming out.

Dust the chops with the flour. Return the skillet to medium-high heat and add the remaining oil. Place the stuffed chops in skillet and brown on both sides. Add the wine, cover, and put into the preheated oven. Bake for 1 hour and 15 minutes, basting at least once. (If chops are thinner, cooking time will be less.) Transfer chops to a platter and keep warm while finishing the sauce. Remove toothpicks if used.

Return skillet to stovetop and bring juices to a simmer over medium heat. Using a wooden spoon, scrape any bits from the bottom of the skillet and simmer until juices are about ½ cup. If necessary, add more wine. Stir in brown sugar, cinnamon, and peach slices; simmer just until peaches are soft but not mushy. Spoon over the chops and serve.

# Parmesan-Crusted Tilapia with Peach Salsa

Serves 4

4 tilapia fillets

Chef Belinda Seafood Spice Blend or salt and lemon pepper, to taste

½ cup grated Parmesan cheese

Peach Salsa (page 141), to taste

*Tilapia is a star no matter how you prepare it. Equally happy to stand on its own as an entrée, the addition of the Peach Salsa brings a slight tanginess that complements the mild, sweet flavor of tilapia. Tilapia is a member of the catfish family, and you can certainly substitute catfish in this recipe.*

Preheat oven to 400 degrees F.

Season fillets on both sides with the spice blend. Pour the Parmesan into a shallow bowl. Dredge fillets in cheese and place on a parchment- or foil-lined baking sheet. Let rest for 30–45 minutes.

Bake the tilapia for 8–10 minutes, until opaque and flaky. Transfer to a serving platter and top with the salsa.

# Spicy Oven Ribs with Peach Barbecue Sauce

1 slab spare ribs or baby back
   ribs

Chef Belinda Grilling Rub
   or your favorite dry rub,
   to taste

Peach Barbecue Sauce
   (page 148)

*The beauty of this recipe is not having to spend hours over a hot grill in the blistering sun. This slow-cooked oven method is beyond easy. Put the ribs in the oven early and let them cook all day. By dinner time, they are fork-tender and perfect.*

Place slab of ribs on a piece of aluminum foil large enough to fold into a packet. Sprinkle the rub over the ribs, rubbing in thoroughly on both sides. With the ribs meat side down, tightly fold the foil to form a sealed packet. Refrigerate overnight if possible to allow meat to absorb flavor.

Preheat oven to 200 degrees F.

Put the rib packet on a rimmed baking sheet and place in oven. Bake for 4 to 6 hours, until a fork easily penetrates the meat. Open the packet, pour off the accumulated juices, and discard the foil. Coat ribs with sauce and allow to rest for 15–30 minutes. Cut and serve. The ribs can also be finished for 2–3 minutes on a hot open grill or under the broiler to create a little charring before coating with sauce.

# Salmon with Peach-Mango Sauce

*Serves 4*

4 salmon fillets

Chef Belinda Seafood Spice Blend, or seafood seasoning or Old Bay, to taste

2 to 3 tablespoons Chile Honey (recipe follows)

Peach-Mango Sauce (page 140)

Chopped fresh dill, for garnish

## CHILE HONEY

3 Thai chiles

1 cup honey

*This is a go-to entrée when time is of the essence. The Chile Honey delivers just the right amount of sweet heat, while keeping the salmon moist, and the mango adds a tropical flavor and a touch of silkiness to the sauce.*

Season the fillets with the spice blend and brush with the Chile Honey. Set aside for 10–15 minutes. Preheat the broiler and arrange a rack in the middle of oven.

In a shallow baking pan lined with aluminum foil, place the salmon fillets under the broiler. Cook for 10 minutes, or until the fillets flake easily when tested with a fork. Remove from oven and transfer to a serving platter. Spoon the sauce over the fillets and garnish with dill.

## CHILE HONEY

Place the chiles in a small jar. In a small saucepan, heat the honey to a temperature of at least 180 degrees F. Pour the warm honey into the jar over the chiles. Let cool to room temperature, cover with a tight lid, and store at room temperature.

# Pies

Pies are entrenched in our society—who doesn't like them? But when we use the term "pie," it brings to mind different things to different people. Brought to our country by early settlers, pies can vary regionally. Thus, we have derived many names for them and how they differ, see page 104. The one thing most agree on is that they all contain fruit (at least the dessert varieties) and some variation of pastry. Oh, and that they are best when served with ice cream!

## PIE

Pastry crust on the bottom, fruit in the middle, and pastry on the top—either fully covering the pie, or in strips, woven together in a lattice. The latter is almost always misrepresented as a "cobbler," which it is not.

## COBBLER

Fruit on the bottom and biscuit dough in pieces on top. The rounds of dough resemble cobblestones when baked. Thus, a cobbler.

## CRISP

Fruit on the bottom and a crispy layer on top. Unlike a crumble, a crisp usually has oatmeal and/or nuts in the topping.

## CRUMBLE

Fruit on the bottom with a crumbly layer of streusel over the top, usually made from only sugar, flour, and butter (unlike the crisp, which contains oats and nuts).

## GRUNT OR SLUMP

Like a cobbler but made on the stovetop in a skillet. Fruit on the bottom and spooned biscuit-style dough on top.

## BETTY OR BROWN BETTY

Layers of fruit and bread pieces or crumbs.

## BUCKLE

Cake-like batter on the bottom and fruit on the top. As it bakes, the fruit settles toward the bottom and is suspended in the cake/dough.

## PANDOWDY

Fruit on the bottom and rolled pastry on the top. Once out of the oven, the pastry is broken into pieces, allowing the edges to absorb the juices.

## TART

Pastry on the bottom *only* with filling on top. Examples are Boston Cream, pecan, or pumpkin pie and cheesecake.

# Pie Crust Dough

2 ½ cups all-purpose flour

½ teaspoon kosher salt

12 tablespoons unsalted butter, cut into ½-inch cubes and chilled

8 tablespoons shortening, chilled and cut into pieces

6 to 8 tablespoons cold water

*This pie crust recipe is so easy to make. The ingredients for making pie crust dough have changed over the years: my grandmother used all shortening for her pie crust, while my mother used half shortening and half butter. On the other hand, I use all butter. Each set of ingredients yields different results, and they are all centered on taste and tenderness. I recommend both shortening and butter here because I want you to get the best possible results. Choose your ingredients preference and stick to it! Additionally, my grandmother would never have used a food processor to make her pie crust dough, but then again, she didn't have access to one.*

Into the bowl of a food processor add the flour and salt; pulse for a few seconds. Add the butter and shortening and pulse until flour takes on a pea-like consistency. Adding the water 2 tablespoons at a time, process until the ingredients form a ball and pull away from the sides of the bowl. Remove dough from food processor. Divide in half and flatten into 2 disks. Wrap in plastic wrap and refrigerate for 1 hour, or up to 2 days.

# Old-Fashioned Peach Pie

8 medium ripe peaches,
peeled and sliced

2 tablespoons cornstarch

1 cup sugar

1 ½ teaspoon ground
cinnamon

1 teaspoon freshly squeezed
lemon juice

1 teaspoon vanilla extract

Pinch of salt

2 (9-inch) pie crusts, store-
bought or homemade (see
page 105)

2 tablespoons unsalted
butter, cut into pieces

*This is the peach pie recipe that my grandmother passed on to my mother and that she would eventually pass on to me. And this is the same peach pie that was always waiting for me on every visit back home. My grandmother made it with a solid crust on top, and my mother made it with a lattice top. Either way, no matter the crust, this pie is downright homemade goodness!!*

Preheat oven to 400 degrees F. In a large bowl, combine the peaches, cornstarch, sugar, cinnamon, lemon juice, vanilla, and salt. Mix thoroughly and set aside.

Take 1 disk of pie dough out of the refrigerator and let rest for 5–10 minutes to make dough easier to roll out. On a dry, well-floured surface, roll out dough to 12 inches, enough to have some overhang all around the pie dish. Place into a 9-inch dish, being careful not to tear the dough. Trim off the excess dough to about a ½-inch overhang all around. Pour the peach mixture into the bottom crust. Dot the top of filling with small pieces of butter.

Roll out the second crust and carefully cover the filling. To make a lattice top, roll out second crust to slightly larger than the top of pie and, using a knife or pizza cutter, cut into strips. Place individual strips on top of fruit, in a woven pattern; or simply place half in one direction and the remaining half in a cross direction. Trim top dough to about a ¾-inch overhang. Tuck top dough edges over and under bottom dough edges and flute the edges all around using your thumbs and forefinger, or crimp with a fork. Using a fork or small, sharp knife, make slits in the top crust so steam can escape and not crack the top crust. Bake for about 45 minutes, until brown and bubbly. Serve warm or room temperature.

# Blueberry-Peach Slump

*Serves 8 to 10*

*One of the many variations of early American pies, the slump, also referred to as a grunt, is essentially a cobbler cooked on top of the stove. The slump can be made with any fruit or combination of fruits. Slumps are gaining significant popularity with the current outdoor open-fire cooking movement, and they are a perfect summer dessert when you don't want to turn on your oven. If you have been looking for ways to use your (well-seasoned) cast iron skillet—especially in outdoor cooking—this is it.*

## FILLING

6 medium peaches, peeled and sliced

1 pint blueberries

½ cup sugar

Pinch of salt

1 tablespoon cornstarch

1 teaspoon Chef Belinda Moroccan Spice Blend or cardamom

1 tablespoon freshly squeezed lemon juice

¼ cup water

## TOPPING

1 cup all-purpose flour

2 tablespoons sugar

½ teaspoon kosher salt

1 teaspoon baking powder

½ teaspoon baking soda

4 tablespoons unsalted butter, cubed and chilled

½ cup buttermilk

## FILLING

In a large bowl combine the peaches, blueberries, sugar, salt, cornstarch, spice blend, lemon juice, and water in a large bowl. Pour into a well-seasoned 9-inch cast iron skillet. Over medium-high heat, bring to a boil. Reduce temperature to medium-low and let simmer while you make the topping.

## TOPPING

In a medium bowl whisk together the flour, sugar, salt, baking powder, and baking soda. Using a pastry cutter, cut in the butter until flour mixture resembles coarse meal. Gradually stir in enough buttermilk until mixture becomes a sticky dough (there may be buttermilk leftover). Do not overmix. Using a spoon, drop spoonfuls of dough evenly over the simmering peach mixture.

Cover and cook for 20 minutes, or until dough has spread and is puffy (springs back when you touch it). Remove the cover and let cool slightly before serving.

# Blackberry-Peach Buckle

*Serves 8 to 10*

2 cups all-purpose flour

2 teaspoons baking powder

½ teaspoon kosher salt

½ teaspoon cardamom

8 tablespoons unsalted butter, room temperature

¾ cup sugar

1 large egg, room temperature

1 teaspoon vanilla extract

½ cup milk

2 to 3 peaches, sliced (peeled or unpeeled)

1 pint blackberries

Confectioners' sugar, for dusting

*The buckle, the almost-forgotten American pie, was the precursor to the coffee cake. While the preparations are similar, a coffee cake will generally be finished on top with a layer of streusel. Not so for the buckle, which is finished with more of whichever fruit for which it is named. Feel free to make this recipe using blueberries, raspberries, or any berries of your choice. For a more rustic presentation, this dish is spectacular when served in a cast iron skillet.*

Preheat oven to 350 degrees F. Spray a 9-inch springform pan with baking spray.

In a medium bowl, combine the flour, baking powder, salt, and cardamom.

In the bowl of a stand mixer, cream the butter until it is a pale yellow. Add the sugar and continue beating until thoroughly mixed. Add the egg and vanilla. Add flour mixture, alternating with the milk, until well-mixed.

Pour the batter into the prepared pan and add the peaches and blackberries, spreading evenly in a pretty design. Bake for 1 hour, or until golden brown and a cake tester inserted into the center comes out clean.

Let cool completely in pan. Remove sides and dust with confectioners' sugar. Serve at room temperature.

# Country Peach Tart

½ cup peach preserves

2 tablespoons water

4 large ripe peaches, peeled and sliced

2 tablespoons brown sugar

1 teaspoon cardamom

1 teaspoon freshly squeezed lemon juice

1 (9-inch) pie crust, store-bought or homemade (see page 105)

2 tablespoons heavy cream or milk

2 tablespoons sugar

Confectioners' sugar, for dusting

*Tarts are the perfect dessert choice when time is of the essence. Easy to prepare, they can be made using any fruit you happen to have on hand.*

Preheat oven to 400 degrees F.

In a medium saucepan over medium-low heat, combine the peach preserves and the water; heat until spreadable. Let cool slightly.

Toss the peaches with the brown sugar, cardamom, and lemon juice.

On a well-floured work surface or wax paper, roll out the pie crust to make a 12-inch circle or rectangle. Transfer to a baking sheet and coat evenly with preserves to about 2 inches from the edge of crust. Mound the peach slices on top of preserves, still maintaining the 2 inches of border around the peaches.

Fold the dough up over the peaches, forming a nest and leaving the center exposed. Brush the exposed crust with the cream and sprinkle with the sugar. Bake for 30 minutes then allow to cool for at least 15 minutes before serving.

Serve with a dusting of confectioners' sugar.

# Raspberry-Peach Crumble

*Serves 8*

## TOPPING

1 cup all-purpose flour

½ cup firmly packed brown sugar

½ cup sugar

1 teaspoon ground cinnamon

Pinch of salt

½ cup unsalted butter, cut into small pieces

## FILLING

6 to 8 peaches, peeled and sliced

1 pint raspberries

Juice of ½ lemon

¼ cup sugar

1 tablespoon cornstarch

*Crumbles are very similar to crisps, with the exception of the topping. A crisp is made with a streusel-like topping and contains nuts and oats. This recipe works well with any berries—blackberries, blueberries, strawberries, boysenberries, cranberries, and cherries. You can even use your favorite grapes.*

Preheat oven to 350 degrees F.

## TOPPING

In a medium bowl, combine the flour, sugars, cinnamon, salt, and butter. Using clean hands, rub together ingredients until mixture sticks together in small clumps.

## FILLING

Arrange the peaches and raspberries in a deep pie dish. Sprinkle with the lemon juice, sugar, and cornstarch; toss thoroughly. Spread the topping evenly over the fruit.

Bake until golden brown and juices are bubbling up through the topping, 45–50 minutes. Serve warm or room temperature.

# Lynne Chappell's "Easy as Pie" Peach Cobbler

Serves 6 to 8

1 cup self-rising flour

1 cup sugar

1 large egg

8 to 10 peaches, depending on size

½ cup unsalted butter, melted

*This recipe is provided by Lynne Chappell of Chappell Farms, a family-owned-and-operated peach farm in Kline, South Carolina.*

Preheat oven to 350 degrees F.

In a medium bowl, mix the flour and sugar together. Add the egg and, using your fingers, knead until crumbly.

Peel and slice the peaches. Place in an 8 x 8-inch baking pan, filling to three-fourths full. Sprinkle the crumb mixture over top of the peaches. Pour the butter over the top.

Bake for 35–40 minutes, until brown on top and bubbly. Watch very closely; do not overcook.

# Desserts

# Peach Bread Pudding
# with Rum Peach Coulis

1 loaf day-old bread (French, Italian, or brioche), cut into 1-inch cubes

3 large eggs

2 ½ cups heavy cream

¾ cups sugar

2 teaspoons vanilla extract

1 teaspoon cardamom

¼ teaspoon kosher salt

3 to 4 peaches, peeled and chopped

½ cup chopped pecans

¼ cup currants or raisins

Rum Peach Coulis (page 143), for serving

*Nothing quite compares to the old-fashioned wholesome goodness of a bread pudding right out of the oven. In this version, the tart currants act as a counterbalance to the sweetness of the peaches.*

Lightly spray a 9 x 13-inch baking dish with nonstick baking spray. Arrange the bread in the dish. In a large bowl, whisk the eggs, cream, sugar, vanilla, cardamom, and salt. Pour liquid mixture over the bread. Cover with plastic wrap and refrigerate overnight to allow bread to absorb the liquid.

Preheat oven to 350 degrees F.

Remove bread pudding from refrigerator; gently toss in the peaches and sprinkle the pecans and currants over the top. Bake for 50–60 minutes, until set in the center and golden brown on top. Allow to rest for 10 minutes before serving. Serve with the coulis.

# Peach Upside-Down Cake

*Serves 8 to 10*

½ cup firmly packed brown sugar

4 tablespoons unsalted butter, melted

½ teaspoon Chef Belinda Caribbean Blend Coffee Spice Mix, or cinnamon or nutmeg

5 to 6 peaches, peeled and sliced

1 ½ cups all-purpose flour

1 teaspoon baking powder

½ teaspoon baking soda

¼ teaspoon kosher salt

½ cup unsalted butter

⅔ cup sugar

1 large egg

1 teaspoon almond extract

1 cup buttermilk

Confectioners' sugar, for dusting

*An all-in-one cake that comes from the oven picture-perfect and ready to eat, this is the cake my grandmother made most often on the farm. Maybe because it required the least amount of work.*

Preheat oven to 350 degrees F. Spray a well-seasoned 9-inch cast iron skillet with nonstick cooking spray.

In a small bowl, combine the brown sugar, melted butter, and spice blend. Pour into the skillet and arrange the peaches on top. Set aside.

In a small bowl, combine the flour, baking powder, baking soda, and salt. In the bowl of a stand mixer, beat the butter and sugar together until pale yellow. Add the egg and almond extract; beat until combined. Lower the mixer speed and alternately add flour mixture and buttermilk; beat until just combined.

Pour mixture into the skillet and spread evenly over the peaches. Bake for 35–45 minutes, until a cake tester inserted into the center comes out clean. Cool for 10 minutes in pan before inverting onto a serving plate. Dust with confectioners' sugar and serve warm.

# Peach-Amaretto Ice Cream

*Makes 1 1/2 quarts*

4 large ripe peaches, peeled
and chopped, divided

1 1/2 tablespoons freshly
squeezed lemon juice

1/2 cup plus 2 tablespoons
sugar, divided

2 tablespoons amaretto

1 1/2 cups heavy cream,
divided

1 1/2 cups whole milk

1 vanilla bean, split and
halved

6 large egg yolks

*This refreshing summer treat is amazing! Always a crowd-pleaser and so effortless to make. It's ice cream—and nothing puts a smile on your face faster.*

In a medium bowl, mash half of the peaches; sprinkle with the lemon juice, 2 tablespoons of the sugar, and amaretto. Cover with plastic wrap and refrigerate.

In a medium heavy-bottom pan, combine 1 cup of the cream, milk, and remaining peaches. Scrape the seeds from the vanilla bean and add both the seeds and the pod to the milk mixture. Cook over medium heat for about 5 minutes, until bubbles start to form around the inside edges of the pan. Strain through a fine sieve, pressing on the peaches with the back of a spoon. Discard the vanilla pod and solids. Pour back into the pan.

In a medium bowl, combine the egg yolks, remaining sugar, and remaining cream; whisk until smooth. Gradually add in 1/2 cup of the hot milk mixture into the egg mixture; then pour all back into the pan. Cook over medium heat, stirring constantly to keep at a simmer, until the custard is thick enough to coat the back of a wooden spoon, about 5 minutes. Do not let the custard boil.

Strain custard through a sieve into a medium bowl to remove the sediment. Place the bowl over a larger bowl filled halfway with water and ice. Stir occasionally to cool. Cover with plastic film, pressing it directly on top of the custard to prevent a skin from forming. Refrigerate for at least 3 hours, or overnight.

Pour custard into an ice cream maker and freeze according to manufacturer's instructions. Add reserved peaches in the last 10 minutes of the churning process. Transfer to a clean freezer-safe container; cover and freeze until firm.

# Oreo-Peach Cheesecake

## CRUST

1 ¾ cups Oreo crumbs

4 tablespoons unsalted
butter, melted

2 tablespoons sugar

## FILLING

3 peaches, peeled and sliced

1 cup plus 2 tablespoons
sugar, divided

1 teaspoon freshly squeezed
lemon juice

4 (8-ounce) packages cream
cheese, room temperature

5 eggs

1 teaspoon vanilla extract or
amaretto

1 teaspoon lemon zest

## GLAZE

½ cup peach preserves or
jam

1 ½ teaspoons freshly
squeezed lemon juice

*Cheesecakes are always a great way to end a meal. When I entertain in the summer, this is my favorite dessert to serve special guests.*

Preheat oven to 350 degrees F.

### CRUST

Combine the Oreos, butter, and sugar. Press mixture firmly against the bottom of a 9-inch springform pan. Wrap the bottom and outside of pan with foil.

### FILLING

Combine the peaches, 2 tablespoons of the sugar, and lemon juice in a medium saucepan. Cook over medium heat until sugar dissolves and peaches are juicy, about 5 minutes. Cool and drain.

In the bowl of a stand mixer, beat the cream cheese until fluffy. Gradually add the remaining sugar. Then add in the eggs, 1 at a time. Add the vanilla and lemon zest, beating until smooth. Pour half of the batter into prepared pan, followed by ⅔ peaches, and top with remaining batter.

Place cheesecake pan inside a larger pan and place in oven. Fill the larger pan halfway with hot water. Bake for 60–70 minutes, until slightly firm in the center. Turn off oven, leaving door ajar about 8 inches, and allow to cool in oven for 1 hour. Remove from oven and cool completely in pan. Chill in refrigerator for 4 hours, or overnight.

### GLAZE

Combine the preserves and lemon juice in a small saucepan over medium heat. Cook, stirring constantly, until it starts to simmer. Using the back of a wooden spoon, strain into a small bowl. Remove sides of springform pan and spread glaze over top of cheesecake followed by remaining peaches. Chill until glaze is set, 2–4 hours.

# Peach-Coconut Cake

*Serves 12 To 16*

## CAKE

- 3 cups all-purpose flour
- 1 tablespoon baking powder
- ½ teaspoon kosher salt
- 1 cup coconut milk or whole milk
- 2 teaspoons vanilla extract
- 2 sticks unsalted butter, room temperature
- 2 cups sugar
- 3 large eggs, room temperature

## FILLING

- 3 peaches, peeled and diced
- ¼ cup sugar
- 1 teaspoon freshly squeezed lemon juice
- 1 tablespoon cornstarch
- 1 ½ tablespoons peach brandy or schnapps

*Coconut cake was my mother's favorite, but she only made it once a year—and that was on her birthday. I would sit and watch intensely as she cracked open the coconut, reserved the coconut milk to add to the cake, and then take what seemed like forever grating the fresh coconut flesh to finish off the cake frosting. The finished cake was a thing of beauty and truly a labor of love. Now, every year, I make a coconut cake in memory of my mother. And although I do take a few shortcuts, it's still a labor of my love for her!*

Preheat oven to 350 degrees F. Spray 2 (9-inch) or 3 (8-inch) cake pans with nonstick baking spray and insert parchment sheets.

### CAKE

Mix together the flour, baking powder, and salt in a medium bowl. In a measuring cup, combine the milk and vanilla. Set both aside.

In the bowl of a stand mixer, cream the butter until it turns pale yellow. Add the sugar and continue beating until thoroughly mixed. Add the eggs, 1 at a time, beating well after each addition and scrape down the sides of the bowl.

Add the flour mixture to the butter mixture, 1 cup at a time, alternating with the milk. Scrape down sides again. Pour into prepared pans.

Bake for 30–35 minutes, until a cake tester inserted into the center comes out clean. Cool in pan for 20 minutes; then invert onto wire racks and let cool completely. Remove parchment sheets.

*Continued*

## FROSTING

2 sticks unsalted butter, room temperature

2 teaspoons vanilla extract

5 cups confectioners' sugar, sifted

1 to 2 tablespoons milk

7 ounces sweetened shredded coconut

## FILLING

Combine the peaches, sugar, and lemon juice in a medium saucepan over medium heat. Bring to a simmer, reduce heat, and let simmer for 15 minutes. In a small bowl, mix the cornstarch and brandy. Add to peaches, stir, and simmer until thick. Let cool.

## FROSTING

Add the butter and vanilla into the bowl of a stand mixer; cream until thoroughly combined and pale yellow. Lower speed and slowly add the sugar until incorporated. Increase mixer speed and beat until smooth. At this point, the frosting may appear a little stiff or dry. Add milk, a little at a time, until frosting is at the proper spreading consistency.

To assemble the cake, use a serrated knife to cut off any domes or humps on your cooled cakes. Put 1 layer on a cake plate and spread with filling, staying about ½ inch from the edges of the cake. If you have 3 layers, repeat with a second layer and more filling, topping with the third layer. Do not put filling on the top layer.

Frost the top of the cake and then the sides. Finish the cake by covering top and sides with shredded coconut. Garnish with additional sliced peaches if desired.

Tip: To prevent the peach filling from spilling over the side of the cake, I use a piping bag fitted with a number 12 piping tip filled with enough of the frosting to pipe a bead around the edge of each filling layer.

# Peach-Walnut Loaf Cake

*Serves 8 to 10*

1 ½ cups all-purpose flour

½ teaspoon salt

1 teaspoon baking soda

½ teaspoon baking powder

6 tablespoons unsalted butter, room temperature

1 cup sugar

2 large eggs

1 teaspoon lemon extract

1 cup peeled and finely diced peaches

¾ cup chopped walnuts

*I don't believe in wasting food. Whenever I have bananas that are beyond eating, they are quickly made into delicious banana bread. Likewise, during the summer, ripe peaches are made into this loaf cake, a modified version of my banana bread recipe.*

Preheat oven to 350 degrees F. Spray a standard loaf pan with nonstick baking spray.

In a medium bowl, whisk together the flour, salt, baking soda, and baking powder.

In the bowl of a stand mixer, cream the butter until it is pale yellow. Add the sugar and continue beating until thoroughly mixed. Add eggs, 1 at a time, beating well after each addition. Add the lemon extract. Add the flour mixture and continue beating until mixed. Fold in the peaches and walnuts.

Pour batter into the prepared loaf pan. Bake for 55 minutes, or until cake tester comes out clean. Cool in pan for 10 minutes; then turn onto a wire rack to cool completely.

# Peach-Thyme Pound Cake

*Serves 12 to 16*

3 cups all-purpose flour

½ teaspoon baking soda

½ teaspoon kosher salt

1 cup unsalted butter, room temperature

2 cups sugar

6 large eggs, room temperature

2 tablespoons almond extract

½ cup sour cream

2 tablespoons chopped fresh thyme

2 cups peeled and diced peaches

Confectioners' sugar, for dusting

*This recipe is an adaptation of my mother's. When I was growing up, pound cake was a staple in our house. It was our favorite dessert, and our family went through at least two per week. My mother was known as the pound cake lady because she baked pound cakes for just about every family on our block, and sometimes it seemed like the whole city. There were always at least two or three pound cakes in our family freezer—my mother was always prepared for whatever occasion might strike!*

Preheat oven to 350 degrees F. Spray a 12-cup bundt pan with nonstick baking spray.

In a medium bowl, whisk together the flour, baking soda, and salt.

In the bowl of a stand mixer, cream the butter until it is pale yellow. Add the sugar and continue beating until thoroughly mixed. Add the eggs, 1 at a time, beating well after each addition. Add the almond extract. Add the flour mixture, 1 cup at a time, alternating with the sour cream. Fold in the thyme and peaches.

Pour batter into prepared pan and bake for 1 hour and 15 minutes, until a cake tester inserted into the center comes out clean. Let cake cool for 15 minutes in the pan; then invert onto a wire rack and let cool completely. Dust with confectioners' sugar, if desired.

# Terry's Peach Dessert Pizza

*Serves 8*

2 (9-inch) pie crusts, store-
bought or homemade
(page 105)

4 tablespoons unsalted
butter, softened

1 (8-ounce) package cream
cheese, room temperature

½ cup sugar, divided

½ teaspoon Chef Belinda
Turkish Blend Coffee
Spice Mix, or cardamom or
cinnamon

½ teaspoon orange extract

3 cups fresh (or frozen or
canned) peach slices

Confectioners' sugar, for
dusting

Whipped cream, for garnish

*This recipe is an adaptation of one shared with me by my friend and
neighbor Terry Bibeau, who loves experimenting with different cake, pie,
and pastry ideas!*

Preheat oven to 350 degrees F.

Lay first pie crust on a floured work surface and spread with the butter.
Lay second crust on top of first, aligning evenly. Using a rolling pin, roll out
to a 12-inch circle. Transfer crust to a large pizza pan or baking sheet. Using
your fingers, roll the outer edge of the crust inward 1 inch to form a raised lip
around the circumference of the crust.

In the bowl of a stand mixer, combine the cream cheese, ¼ cup of the sugar,
spice mix, and orange extract; beat until smooth. Spread evenly on top of
crust and press peach slices into mixture in an evenly spaced pattern. Sprinkle
the remaining ¼ cup sugar on top of peaches.

Bake for 30–40 minutes, until crust is golden brown and peaches and
cream cheese are bubbly. Let cool for 15 minutes. Sprinkle with confectioners'
sugar. Slice and serve with a dollop of whipped cream. Refrigerate leftovers.

# Chocolate-Peach Soufflé

*Makes 6 6-ounce ramekins*

2 tablespoons unsalted butter, softened (plus more as needed)

2 tablespoons superfine (caster) sugar

1 large peach, peeled and chopped small

7 ounces 70-percent dark chocolate, finely chopped

½ cup heavy cream

3 tablespoons peach brandy, peach schnapps, or peach extract

2 large eggs, separated

3 large egg whites

6 tablespoons sugar, divided

Pinch of salt

Confectioners' sugar, for dusting

*These individual-size soufflés will impress even the most hardened dessert critics. And finding that little peach surprise waiting at the bottom of the dish—the perfect ending. Soufflés are easy to make if you adhere to a few simple rules: be sure to thoroughly coat the ramekins with butter and sugar, beat the egg whites until stiff, and gently fold the chocolate and egg whites together. To be consumed at their best, soufflés should be served right out of the oven.*

Preheat oven to 375 degrees F. Grease each ramekin with the butter, and completely coat the insides with sugar. Add 2 tablespoons peaches to each ramekin. Place ramekins on a sheet pan and set aside.

Place the chocolate in a medium bowl. Combine the cream and brandy in a small saucepan over medium-low heat and bring just to a simmer. Pour hot cream over chocolate and let sit for 1 minute; then stir until smooth and glossy. Add the egg yolks, stir again, and set aside.

In the bowl of a stand mixer, using the whisk attachment, beat the 5 egg whites with 1 tablespoon of the sugar and the salt until frothy. Increase speed and continue to beat, gradually adding sugar, 1 tablespoon at a time, until peaks form and egg whites cling to the whisk. Do not overbeat.

Using a spatula, gently fold the chocolate mixture into the whites. Fill the ramekins with the mixture and bake for 15–20 minutes, until they puff up and are set. Test in the center with a cake tester, which should come out clean. Dust with confectioners' sugar and serve immediately.

# Peach-Filled Kolachkes

*Makes 7 dozen cookies*

12 ounces cream cheese, room temperature

1 pound (4 sticks) unsalted butter, room temperature

4 cups all-purpose flour

Confectioners' sugar, for rolling out

1 ½ cups peach preserves

*When we were small children, the tradition in our house on Christmas Eve was to bake these cookies for Santa. We would leave them on the coffee table next to the Christmas tree along with a small glass of brandy. The first thing we would do when we woke up on Christmas morning was to check to see if he had eaten our goodies! The cookies were always gone, but the brandy would still be there. The three of us would sneak over and take a sip before our parents woke up. I've often wondered if they ever realized we did that.*

*These cookies are so easy to make, even the youngest kids will have fun helping. This recipe makes a generous seven dozen cookies, but feel free to cut in half or quarter. The dough will also freeze well for up to three months. This is an excellent choice for your cookie swaps.*

In the bowl of a stand mixer, beat together the cream cheese and butter. Lower speed on mixer and add the flour, a little at a time, until well-mixed. Divide the dough into 4 portions. Wrap each portion in plastic wrap and refrigerate overnight.

Preheat oven to 350 degrees F.

Sprinkle a clean, dry work surface and rolling pin with confectioners' sugar. Working with one portion at a time, roll out the dough to about ¼ inch thick. Use a 2-inch round cookie or biscuit cutter to cut out cookies. Place on an ungreased baking sheet, leaving 2 inches between each cookie. Using your thumb, make an indentation on the top of each cookie and add about ¼ teaspoon peach preserves. Do not use too much or it will run off onto the baking sheet.

Alternatively, you can use a 2-inch square cookie cutter. Put ½ teaspoon preserves on each square, and fold two diagonally opposite sides over the filling to enclose.

Bake until bottoms are golden brown, about 20 minutes.

# Sauces & Condiments

# Peach-Mango Sauce

½ cup firmly packed brown
   sugar

2 teaspoons Dijon mustard

1 teaspoon minced fresh
   ginger

2 teaspoons freshly squeezed
   orange juice

1 teaspoon cornstarch

2 peaches, peeled and diced

2 mangoes, peeled and diced

*If your taste leans more to sweet than tart and spicy, this sauce is for you. It goes best with fish and pork. Easy to prepare, the sauce cooks up quickly on the stovetop while the meat is in the oven.*

In a medium skillet, mix together the brown sugar, mustard, ginger, orange juice, and cornstarch; bring to a boil over medium-low heat. Simmer for 5 minutes, stirring occasionally. Add the peaches and mangoes and simmer for an additional 3–4 minutes. Remove from heat and keep warm. Store any leftovers in a covered container in the refrigerator for up to 1 week.

# Peach Salsa

2 cups chopped peaches

1 red bell pepper, diced

½ red onion, diced

2 tablespoons chopped fresh cilantro

1 tablespoon chopped mint

2 tablespoons freshly squeezed lime juice

1 tablespoon honey

Pinch of red pepper flakes

*This sweet and tangy sauce is a great accompaniment to any meat, especially baked chicken, grilled pork chops, or fish.*

In a medium bowl, thoroughly combine the peaches, bell pepper, onion, cilantro, mint, lime juice, honey, and pepper flakes. Cover and refrigerate until ready to use. Store any leftovers in a covered container in the refrigerator for up to 1 week.

# Spicy Peach-Jalapeño Salsa

4 cups diced peaches

2 jalapeños, seeds and veins removed, diced

½ red onion, diced

Pinch of red pepper flakes

¼ cup freshly squeezed lime juice

¼ cup chopped fresh cilantro

*Peach salsa with a kick! Use on meats when extra heat is desired. It really enhances the flavor of grilled pork chops and tenderloins. Try it with your favorite Tex-Mex meals.*

In a medium bowl, combine the peaches, jalapeños, onion, pepper flakes, lime juice, and cilantro. Mix well and refrigerate until ready to use. Store any leftovers in a covered container in the refrigerator for up to 1 week.

# Rum Peach Coulis

½ cup water

1 cup sugar

2 cups chopped peaches

1 mint leaf

1 tablespoon white rum

*This peach coulis is an easy fruit sauce that enhances the flavor and presentation of cakes, pies, brownies, ice cream, waffles, and other desserts.*

In a medium saucepan over medium heat, bring the water and sugar to a boil; stir until sugar is dissolved. Increase temperature to medium-high and add the peaches and mint. When peaches start to boil, reduce heat to medium-low and simmer, stirring occasionally, until peaches start to soften, 10–15 minutes.

Remove pan from heat and stir in the rum. Let cool for about 15 minutes. Using the back of a spoon, mash the peach mixture through a fine-mesh sieve into a clean bowl. Discard the pulp. Transfer coulis to a small jar and refrigerate for up to 1 week.

# Peach Mustard

Makes about 1 1/2 cups

2 very ripe peaches, peeled and chopped

1 tablespoon honey

1 tablespoon white wine vinegar

½ cup Dijon mustard

½ cup whole grain mustard

Chef Belinda Grains of Paradise, freshly ground, to taste, or a mix of equal parts freshly ground pepper and cardamom, to taste

*When peaches and mustard come together, something magical happens. Suddenly you have a spread that can not only enhance the flavor of grilled meats and vegetables, but also can be slathered on hot dogs, burgers, and sandwiches or used as a dipping sauce for appetizers.*

Place the peaches in a blender and purée until smooth. Add the honey, vinegar, and mustards; season with Grains of Paradise. Pulse a few times to thoroughly combine. Transfer to a clean, dry jar and refrigerate. Store any leftovers in a covered container in the refrigerator for up to 2 months.

# Savory Bourbon Peach Sauce

*Makes about 1 1/2 cups*

1 cup peach preserves

3 tablespoons bourbon

2 tablespoons
   Worcestershire sauce

2 tablespoons Dijon mustard

1/4 teaspoon cayenne pepper

4 tablespoons unsalted
   butter

*This savory sauce is for meats like chicken, pork, or beef. It would not be recommended for desserts.*

In a medium saucepan over medium heat, combine the preserves, bourbon, Worcestershire, mustard, cayenne, and butter. Simmer for about 3 minutes, stirring until butter melts. Let cool, transfer to a jar with a lid, and refrigerate. Store any leftovers in a covered container in the refrigerator for up to 2 months.

# Homemade Peach-Orange Marmalade

4 pounds ripe peaches
(about 5 large peaches),
peeled and chopped

1 orange, thinly sliced,
quartered, and seeds
removed

4 cups sugar

*Marmalades are soft fruit spreads that contain a citrus. Because the entire citrus fruit is used, except the seeds, it produces its own natural pectin, making the addition of commercial pectin unnecessary in the production of marmalade.*

Preheat oven to 225 degrees F.

Combine the peaches, orange, and sugar in a large saucepan; stir over medium heat until sugar is dissolved. Increase heat and cook rapidly until clear and thick, stirring frequently to prevent sticking, 30–40 minutes. (Cooking time will vary with degree of ripeness and type of peach.)

Place 5 half-pint (8-ounce) glass jars on a baking sheet and put in oven for 10 minutes. Put lids and rings in a pot of boiling water for 5 minutes. Leave them in water until ready to cap jars.

Remove marmalade from heat and skim off any foam. Immediately fill the hot, sterilized jars with cooked marmalade, leaving a ½-inch headspace. Make sure to stir up the marmalade as you go so the fruit remains evenly distributed. Apply the lids and rings and wipe clean.

For the next step, if you do not have a canning pot with a canning rack insert, use canning tongs and a large Dutch oven or saucepan with a makeshift rack. This can be a small wire rack that will fit inside the pan or a folded kitchen towel. Just make sure the jars do not sit directly on the bottom of the pan.

In a canning pot, heat water until boiling and immerse jars for 10 minutes. Remove to a dry kitchen towel. Leave jars undisturbed for at least 12 hours before checking the seals. (You may occasionally hear popping sounds; that is the sound of the jars sealing.) Holding jars at eye level, if the top center of the jar is slightly depressed, the jar is properly sealed—if slightly raised, it is not properly sealed. Sealed jars will store up to 1 year. Unsealed jars should be refrigerated and consumed within 1 week.

# Peach Purée

12 very ripe peaches, peeled
and cut into large chunks

¼ cup simple syrup (optional
if peaches are not sweet)

*There are many uses for peach purée, yet it's not always easy to find in the supermarket. Making your own when peaches are abundant will guarantee that you always have a supply on hand when you need it. Use it in mixed drinks, on top of pancakes, in cakes, stirred into yogurt, or to make peach butter; it will become your replacement for applesauce. Peach purée will keep in the refrigerator for up to a week but can be frozen for up to three months.*

Place the peaches and syrup into the bowl of a food processor or blender. Process until smooth. Strain through a sieve, using the back of a spatula or spoon to press on the peaches. Discard solids accumulated in the sieve. Pour purée into clean jars or a pitcher with a lid. Store in the refrigerator or freezer.

Tip: If freezing, freeze first in ice cube trays; then store ice cubes in ziplock freezer bags. Use as needed.

# Peach Barbecue Sauce

*Makes about 1 quart*

¼ cup canola oil

1 Vidalia or sweet onion, chopped

3 cloves garlic, chopped

6 medium peaches, peeled and chopped

¾ cup firmly packed brown sugar

½ cup apple cider vinegar

¼ cup bourbon or water

½ cup Worcestershire sauce

½ cup tomato sauce

½ teaspoon red pepper flakes

½ tablespoon chili powder

Kosher salt and freshly ground black pepper, to taste

Juice from ½ lemon

*This is a refreshing change from your usual barbecue sauce for ribs, chicken, and hamburgers. You can also use it as a dipping sauce for fried chicken tenders and shrimp.*

In a large saucepan over medium-low heat, warm the oil. Add the onion and cook, stirring occasionally, until tender, about 10 minutes. Add the garlic and cook for 1 minute. Stir in the peaches, brown sugar, vinegar, and bourbon. Bring to a boil over high heat, and then reduce the heat to medium. Add the Worcestershire, tomato sauce, pepper flakes, and chili powder; season with salt and pepper. Simmer, uncovered, stirring occasionally, until the peaches and onion are very tender, about 30 minutes. Stir in the lemon juice, remove from heat, and let cool.

Working in batches, transfer the peach mixture to a blender and purée until smooth. Pour into clean jars with lids and refrigerate for up to 2 weeks.

# Peach-Pepper Relish

*Use this relish to enhance the flavor of your favorite fish and shrimp dishes.*

1 ½ cups peeled and chopped peaches

1 cup chopped red bell pepper

¼ cup thinly sliced green onions

1 clove garlic, minced

¼ cup freshly squeezed lemon juice

1 tablespoon chopped fresh cilantro

1 ½ tablespoons chopped fresh mint

¼ teaspoon salt

½ serrano pepper, seeded and minced

In a medium bowl, thoroughly combine all the ingredients. Cover and refrigerate until ready to serve. Store any leftovers in a covered container in the refrigerator for up to 1 month.

# Peach Simple Syrup

2 cups water

2 cups sugar

2 cups peeled and chopped peaches

1 tablespoon freshly squeezed lemon juice

*Simple syrup is equal parts water and sugar boiled down to make a sweet liquid that can be dissolved quickly in beverages where sugar is needed, such as iced tea, lemonade, and mixed drinks.*

Into a medium saucepan over medium-low heat, add the water, sugar, and peaches. Simmer, stirring occasionally, until peaches are tender, 15–20 minutes. Strain through a sieve, using the back of a wooden spoon to mash the peach juices through the sieve into the syrup. Discard the peach pulp. Stir the lemon juice into the syrup and pour into an airtight bottle and refrigerate. This mixture should keep for several weeks.

# Peach Vinaigrette

1 peach, peeled and chopped

¼ cup white wine vinegar

¼ cup extra virgin olive oil

1 tablespoon honey

Kosher salt and freshly ground black pepper, to taste

*A light, fruity dressing that will add a refreshing taste to your summer salads.*

In a blender, purée the peaches. Add the vinegar, olive oil, and honey. Season with salt and pepper and pulse until smooth. Pour into a clean jar with lid and store in refrigerator for up to 1 week.

# Beverages

# Sparkling Peach-Blueberry Lemonade

*Makes about 1 1/2 gallon*

8 to 10 peaches, peeled and diced

½ pint blueberries

2 cups sugar

2 cups water

2 cups freshly squeezed lemon juice

4 cups sparkling water or club soda, chilled

Peach slices, for garnish

½ pint blueberries, for garnish

Lemon wedges, for garnish

Mint sprigs, for garnish

*Who in the peach-producing South doesn't like lemonade? It's definitely a conversation starter and, at the very least, the polite thing to offer a stranger that just happens upon your front porch on a sunny afternoon. Manners matter! This lemonade is just as good made with blackberries, raspberries, and cherries.*

In a large saucepan over medium heat, combine the peaches, blueberries, sugar, and water; bring to a boil. Cook until fruit is soft, stirring occasionally. Let cool slightly.

Using the back of a spoon, press and strain pulp through a fine-mesh sieve into a clean bowl. Discard pulp. Pour the liquid into a pitcher and add lemon juice and sparkling water. Serve lemonade in glasses over ice. Garnish with peaches, blueberries, lemon, and mint.

# Perfectly Simple Peach Iced Tea

4 ice tea bags

8 cups water, divided

1 cup Peach Simple Syrup
  (page 150)

2 peaches, peeled and sliced

Mint sprigs, for garnish

*Nothing is as refreshing during the heat of summer as iced tea. Ask any Southerner and they'll set you straight—it has to be sweet!*

Place tea bags in a large pitcher with a lid. In a kettle, heat 4 cups of the water. Pour hot water over tea bags and cover. Let steep for 15 minutes. Add the syrup and stir. Add remaining water. Serve over ice and garnish with peach slices and mint sprigs.

# Bellini Cocktail

Mint leaves, to taste

2 ounces Peach Purée (page 147)

4 ounces sparkling wine (such as Prosecco, Champagne, or Cava)

1 peach slice, for garnish

*The Bellini is the drink that defines the brunch culture. It brings sparkling wine face to face with the peach—a winning combination. The Bellini originated in the 1940s at Harry's Bar in Venice, Italy—a popular haunt for American writers of that era. Serve it "straight up," without ice. Stirred and not shaken, please!*

Crush a few mint leaves with your fingers and drop into a chilled champagne flute. Add the purée followed by the sparkling wine and gently stir. Garnish with a peach slice if desired.

# Peachy Strawberry-Kiwi Sangria

3 peaches, peeled and sliced

1 ½ cups sliced strawberries

2 kiwis, peeled and sliced

½ cup peach schnapps or brandy

3 tablespoons sugar

1 (750 ml) bottle white wine, chilled

2 cups sparkling water or club soda, chilled

Lemon wedges, for garnish

*A refreshing, fruity drink to serve a crowd or take along on a picnic or warm-weather tailgating. Feel free to change it up with any of your favorite fruits.*

In a pitcher, combine the peaches, strawberries, and kiwis. Pour the schnapps over fruit and sprinkle with sugar. Cover and refrigerate for 2 hours or overnight.

Stir in the wine and sparkling water. Serve over ice and garnish with lemon wedges.

# Granddad's Easy Homemade Peach Brandy

*Makes about 2 quarts*

12 medium peaches, unpeeled (about 5 pounds)

5 pounds sugar

4 tablespoons Saf-Instant dry yeast

Purified water, spring water, or well water (unchlorinated)

*Nothing went to waste on the farm. My grandfather used the peach peels and pits—leftover from peeling peaches to make preserves—to make his version of this brandy. If you do a lot of canning and have an abundance of peels and pits leftover, then by all means turn them into some delicious homemade brandy. A 1- or 3-gallon crock with a lid and weights will come in handy.*

Wash the peaches well and cut out any bad spots. Cut each peach into quarters, reserving the pits. Whisk together the sugar and yeast. Layer the peaches, pits, and sugar mixture alternately in a sterilized crock. Add enough water to the crock to completely cover the peaches.

Place the crock on a shallow tray or pan large enough to catch any spillover from the fermentation process. Place crock weights on top of the peaches, or weight with a plate. Cover the crock with the lid and store in a cool, dark place, preferably a closet or pantry.

Let the crock set, undisturbed, for 1 week. Uncover, remove the weights, and stir using a long-handled spoon. Replace the weights, cover, and let set for an additional 4 weeks, stirring once a week. Strain the mixture several times through a cheesecloth-lined sieve to remove pulp and pits; repeat until all sediment has been removed.

Pour the brandy into sterilized jars or bottles, cover tightly, and store in a cool, dark place for 5–6 months.

# Peach Passion Cocktail

1 ½ ounces Jameson Black Barrel Irish Whiskey

1 ounce freshly squeezed lime juice

5 ounces Peach Simple Syrup (page 150)

3 dashes Peychaud's Bitters

2 ounces Fever Tree Ginger Beer, or ginger beer of choice

Peach slice, for garnish

Lime wedge, for garnish

*This recipe was developed for me by my friend Kelly MacVean to honor the publishing of this book.*

   In a cocktail shaker or small measuring cup, combine the whiskey, lime juice, syrup, bitters, and ginger beer. Pour over ice and garnish with the peach and/or lime.

# Peach Margarita

Rim salt

2 ounces tequila

1 ounce triple sec

1 ounce cognac

1 ounce freshly squeezed lime
  juice

¼ cup Peach Purée (see
  page 147)

1 peach slice, for garnish

*What Mexican, Tex-Mex, or barbeque food celebration would be complete
without margaritas? Bring on the guacamole, salsa, and chips and let's get
this party started!*

Salt the rim of a chilled margarita glass.

In a blender, add the tequila, triple sec, cognac, lime juice, and peach purée.
Blend and pour over ice into the glass. Garnish with a peach slice.

Tip: For a frozen margarita, add 1–2 cups of ice to the blender.

# Index

# Author Bio

Belinda Smith-Sullivan is a chef, food writer, spice blends entrepreneur, and a commercially-rated pilot. She has a culinary arts degree from Johnson & Wales University, and writes a monthly column for both *South Carolina Living* and *Bella Magazine*. She also is featured on *South Carolina Living's* website with monthly how-to videos. Smith-Sullivan is an active member of the Southern Foodways Alliance, International Association of Culinary Professionals, American Culinary Federation, Association of Food Journalists, International Food Wine Travel Writers Association, and Les Dames d'Escoffier. She lives in Trenton, SC, in the heart of South Carolina's peach country.

# Metric Conversion Chart

| VOLUME MEASUREMENTS | | WEIGHT MEASUREMENTS | | TEMPERATURE CONVERSION | |
|---|---|---|---|---|---|
| U.S. | Metric | U.S. | Metric | Fahrenheit | Celsius |
| 1 teaspoon | 5 ml | ½ ounce | 15 g | 250 | 120 |
| 1 tablespoon | 15 ml | 1 ounce | 30 g | 300 | 150 |
| ¼ cup | 60 ml | 3 ounces | 90 g | 325 | 160 |
| ⅓ cup | 75 ml | 4 ounces | 115 g | 350 | 180 |
| ½ cup | 125 ml | 8 ounces | 225 g | 375 | 190 |
| ⅔ cup | 150 ml | 12 ounces | 350 g | 400 | 200 |
| ¾ cup | 175 ml | 1 pound | 450 g | 425 | 220 |
| 1 cup | 250 ml | 2 ¼ pounds | 1 kg | 450 | 230 |